FIRST GRADE

READING PROGRAMS

Compiled and edited by

JAMES F. KERFOOT

The Pennsylvania State University

Prepared by a Committee
of the
International Reading Association

74093

ROBERT KARLIN, Chairman, Publications Committee

JAMES F. KERFOOT, Conference Chairman

International Reading Association
Newark, Delaware 19711

1965

FOREWORD

WITHIN the pages of this fifth volume in the Perspectives in Reading series, Professor Kerfoot and his distinguished group of contributors have presented a clear description—and in most cases an evaluation—of the many approaches now being used to teach reading in the first grade. Anyone wishing to understand current philosophies of reading instruction will find this book a valuable and revealing source of information.

The reader who disdains controversy or who knows that there is only one way to teach reading will find this book a disturbing experience. A brief examination of the table of contents alone indicates that this book does not "take sides." Rather it provides many points of view with final conclusions left to the reader.

This is a timely and significant book. It merits, and will receive, I am sure, wide circulation and careful study.

THEODORE CLYMER
President, 1964-65
International Reading Association

The International Reading Association attempts, through its publications, to provide a forum for a wide spectrum of opinion on reading. This policy permits divergent viewpoints without assuming the endorsement of the Association.

CONTENTS

Page

1. An Overview 1
   James F. Kerfoot

2. Individualized Reading 7
   Patrick Groff

3. Basal Reading 28
   William D. Sheldon

4. Linguistic Approaches 45
   Charles C. Fries

5. Phonic Approaches 56
   Arthur W. Heilman

6. New Alphabet Approaches 72
   Edward Fry

7. Language Experience Approach 86
   Russell G. Stauffer

8. Early Letter Emphasis 119
   John C. Manning

9. Linguistic Approach for the Bilingual 132
   Ralph F. Robinett

10. Programs for the Culturally Disadvantaged 150
    Millard H. Black

11. Standards for Evaluation 173
    Guy L. Bond

JAMES F. KERFOOT

THE PENNSYLVANIA STATE UNIVERSITY

1. First Grade Reading Programs: An Overview

THE PERSPECTIVES IN READING conferences of the International Reading Association have been directed each year toward special topical areas, age groups or issues of current concern. The fifth conference has focused sharply and intensively on the narrow but crucial issue of first grade reading problems and first grade reading programs. The papers in this publication are the collected manuscripts of that conference.

Reading instruction in the first grade is unique in several ways:

First, instructional emphasis is on beginning reading, on phase 1, on the first formal steps of a lifelong developing literacy. Since a child's initial experiences with reading can influence his later reactions to it, the challenge of beginning reading instruction is indisputable. So, too, are the problems.

Second, the developmental characteristics of first grade children add considerably to the teacher's task. She must attempt to motivate and provide experiences for children who are not much bigger than their attention spans and whose motivations are often somewhat less than academic. First grade pupils are inclined to take a good deal more interest in the other children than in the learning task.

Third, the first grade teacher may be overwhelmed by the variety of materials and programs which claim to provide the most appropriate learning experiences and at the same time capture the interest and drive of these small energy burners.

The first grade teacher must therefore be a truly remarkable person and deserves our heartiest applause and all the help that we can provide in the way of research results and the experiences of successful practice. The papers which follow are a valuable contribution to that end.

Teachers have been getting some exposure to first grade reading innovations but not enough comparative exposure. Comparative evaluation is essential because authors and publishers are becoming increasingly persuasive in an age of market analysis and advertising technique.

This conference does not intend to sell materials and programs but to evaluate them. For this reason, we have enlisted the aid of a group of reading persons of the highest professional character—individuals who are willing to present a point of view to which they are substantially committed and at the same time discuss fairly and impartially similar but competing approaches within their topical frames of reference.

However, we are not unwilling to observe bias for two reasons:

First. The papers presented at this conference represent primarily a professional position and only incidentally a commercial one.

Second. The perspectives presented here must withstand the penetrating challenge of discussant analysis, and audience reaction, and in addition, the context of other well articulated, contrasting approaches.

Traditionally, we avoid discussing materials and focus on methodology. However, current methods have become so thoroughly integrated with materials that it is impossible to effectively evaluate reading programs without reference to the materials which function as the major instructional vehicle.

If materials are to be evaluated in terms of a particular type of first grade program, we must make every effort as speakers, discussants, and audience to evaluate at the highest possible professional level. The purpose of the Perspectives Conference is to present perspectives! This we wish to do without taking on the character of a bookman's debate.

Overlap will be observed in the topical content of several papers, but the perspectives differ. Overlap of this type is not to be deplored but, rather, encouraged. Where differing points of view converge on a single program or set of materials, we have the most valuable kind of illumination—that which leads us hopefully to observe with the five blind men that there is more than one side to the elephant.

Individualized reading approaches are discussed by Patrick Groff. Individualized reading has long been at issue among reading people. Intensity of feeling has in recent years abated as the importance of self selection and pacing have been internalized by most authorities. Few structured reading programs today would not include a substantial element of self selection and some even advocate individual conferences in conjunction with more traditional group activities. Conversely, skill development has been receiving greater emphasis in individualized programs. "Emphasis" may be the key word today to distinguish individualized from structured programs.

Dr. Groff has skillfully considered the philosophical and practical values of individualized reading.

Basal reading programs still represent the overwhelming majority of current practice. It is easy to lose sight of that fact because most of the "noise" comes from the other approaches. The carefully systematized materials of the basal program dominate the reading scene and for the first grade teacher typically include in formidable array: two or three readiness workbooks, three or four pre-primers, a primer, a first reader, and transitional materials, not to mention a variety of manuals, workbooks and special materials. In fairness to the basal program which absorbs most of the criticism, it should be added that the manuals characteristically include recommendations and instructions for integrating basal materials with recreational reading, language experience activities, activity games, and other curricular experiences. William Sheldon has admirably expressed the basal position.

The term *linguistic* is a relatively new one in the working vocabulary of the reading teacher. Linguistic approaches have connoted for many teachers some new and secret formula for the teaching of reading, and they have patiently awaited the day of translation. Linguistic science is far from new but the linguist's concern with the teaching of reading may perhaps be viewed as a recent development. The linguists, as language scientists, are having a significant impact on reading instruction. This has been partly due to our dissatisfaction with the present state of reading instruction and our willingness to reach out to a respected group of scientists who offer us a new perspective, new possibilities, or maybe a brand-new formula. A major linguistic contribution has been the redefinition of a rather loose set of educational practices under some unifying principles. The linguists provide us with a vocabulary to describe and a science to prescribe the linguistic content of reading. The two areas of reading of most concern to linguists have been word regularity and sentence structure. These concerns have resulted in the application of the principle of minimal contrast to the introduction of new words and the search for and application of natural language structures in the development of materials. The linguistic position is stripped of some of its mystery in the straight-forward presentation by the eminent linguist, Charles C. Fries.

There are many approaches to reading instruction which may be weighed and considered dispassionately. For each of us there are some approaches that we wish to appraise but do not get particularly excited about. That is, we can take them or leave them. This is surely not the case with phonics. Whatever our present disposition in reading, we tend to get emotional about phonics. We cry that it is not being taught in the schools today, or we insist with equal enthusiasm that it is, or we may say that it is not being taught adequately, or that the wrong phonic approach is being used, or that phonics should be introduced earlier, or that consonants should be introduced before vowels, or that vowels should be introduced before consonants, or that generalizations should be reduced or abandoned. No conscientious teacher of reading can escape the disturbing conflict among phonic committments. Has phonics caused most of the ills of reading instruction? Or is phonics the means to our salvation? What is and should be the role of phonics in a sound reading program? To place phonics in proper perspective and to describe and evaluate a number of phonic emphasis approaches has been the adroitly handled task of Arthur W. Heilman.

New alphabet approaches have captured the imagination of both lay and professional people today. Control of orthography has long been the dream of many who see the English language as a hopeless potpourri of inconsistency. Benjamin Franklin and George Bernard Shaw were just two of the many people concerned over the irregularity of English. The improbability that the English language ever could or will be changed is obvious. On the other hand, the likelihood that inconsistency of grapheme-phoneme correspondence may contribute to reading failure makes some sort of control desirable. While not a new idea, there has been a current resurgence of interest in temporary control of the language for the initial stages of instruction. The various approaches to alphabet control have been described by Edward Fry together with his skillful evaluation of problems and promises.

Because reading is one of the language arts, a mighty struggle has been made to find better ways to take advantage of language arts interrelationships. Early in the history of reading instruction the language arts approach was recognized as an important instructional vehicle. The experience chart approach of yesterday has given way to the language-experience approach of today. The current approach is not revolutionary but has evolved rather naturally from an experience chart base. The differences are best characterized by a shift in emphasis from group to individual experience. While the records of group experience are still an important part of the current approach, must greater emphasis is given today to individual self-expression. The experience chart libraries of thirty years ago have been replaced by classrooms overflowing with the current written work of individual children. The language-experience approach has been well accepted in most classrooms as either the major component or an important adjunct to the reading program. A surprisingly full description of the language experience approach was presented in 1943 by Grace Fernald. Recently wide acclaim has been given to the methods used by Sylvia Ashton-Warner in teaching the Maori children of New Zealand to read. The Ashton-Warner method was a language experience approach greatly similar to that published by Fernald twenty years before. In this volume the language-experience approach has been expertly discussed by Russell Stauffer.

Many attempts have been made to predict success in reading from various readiness measures. One of the most consistently effective predictors of success in reading at the first grade level has been knowledge of letter names. This may be an outgrowth of the unique background or home environment of the child who comes to school already knowing the letters of the alphabet, or perhaps success in learning the alphabet merely indicates certain discrimination and/or association abilities. It has not thus far been clear whether or not direct alphabet instruction would increase reading achievement. Much current interest has been generated in evaluating the effects of an early letter instructional emphasis. The nature and effectiveness of early letter emphasis approaches have been clearly and responsibly presented by John C. Manning.

Programs for bi-lingual children are discussed by Ralph Robinett. With a strong linguistic orientation, Dr. Robinett discusses the teaching of reading to children who have minimal English language experience and who have some experience with a competing second language. While this presentation is primarily an evaluation of methods and materials for children of bilingual backgrounds, it should be carefully considered as a valuable approach for normal background children.

The culturally disadvantaged child, currently in the public eye, has not suddenly been thrust upon us. He has been with us all along, but he is enjoying a new awareness and a new concern for his identification and learning. Millard Black points out that there are many forms of disadvantage or difference which must be accommodated if reading instruction is to be effective with this group As the linguists have suggested, the reading process involves the decoding of symbols representative of previously mastered language structures. There are many children for whom language and conceptual backgrounds must not be assumed. The identification of background deficiencies and the provision of appropriate experiences for such children are the subject of an insightful and provocative discussion by Mr. Black.

Guy L. Bond has accepted the very difficult responsibility of evaluating the papers for this conference. Dr. Bond has first laid down important criteria by which any reading program should be evaluated. Second, the conference was evaluated in terms of the contributions of the various approaches to beginning reading instruction. Each approach was carefully considered in relation to the following characteristics:

1. The rationale for the program.

2. The description of the program indicating elements of uniqueness or emphasis in method, materials, or organization.

3. The current status of the program including research support for the program in general and research information on the effectiveness of the program with different groups of children (bright, dull, average, boys, girls, etc.).

4. The research in progress.

5. The prognosis for the program.

Third, the present status of comparative research projects on first grade reading programs was discussed. In his evaluation, Dr. Bond has done a splendid job of unifying this multi-perspective project.

This volume may appear to raise more questions than it answers. However, much supporting commonality will be evident to the discerning reader. On a number of questions the most defensible current answer must still be that the question remains. The manuscripts presented here may jolt somewhat our familiar and comfortable perspectives. *Viva La Difference!*

PATRICK GROFF

SAN DIEGO STATE COLLEGE

2. Individualized Reading in First Grade

MODERN SCHOOL PROGRAMS designed for the individualization of instruction have come to assume something of a common rationale. In this writer's opinion the point of view of individualization is most convincingly brought forth by two recent publications of two eminent educational study groups (2, 29). As described there, the basis for individualized teaching rests on the evidence found on individual differences. The research literature on this matter, both among individuals and within individuals, seems clear at this point and striking in its importance (36). It shows, roughly, that it is not unusual to be able to double the grade at which one teaches to predict approximately the range of educational achievement to be found there. Thus, in grade four (times two) there might well be eight years in range of educational attainment. There is ordinarily found at least a range of three years in true reading ability at the end of grade one. What is more, this research indicates that the scores individuals make on different sections of achievement tests represent a great variability in the conceptual and informational framework of the individual.

Consequently, as the result of the widespread knowledge of such differences among educators, it would be difficult to find a school system that does not accept the idea that individual differences should in some way govern patterns of instruction. While many teachers may not completely recognize the extent of these differences,* they, too, have been conscious that children exhibit great differences which are reflected in varied rates of learning.

Many attempts have been made to give attention to these differences. In the past attempts to achieve individualization have usually rested on

---

*Goodlad (16), for example, found that fourth grade teachers over-estimated by 20 per cent the number of children in their classes that were achieving precisely at the fourth grade level.

the assumption that there exists a fixed body of subject matter or skills which generally can be found in a graded textbook. Individualization was thought of primarily in terms of how fast a child could learn this subject matter or these skills. With this belief, the teacher's major concern with individualization was, of course, with the rate with which the individual child progressed through this textbook material. Terman said at one time that the school should "measure out the work for each child in proportion to his mental ability." The early writings of Preston Search, Frederic Burk, Carleton Washborne (the Winnetka Plan); Helen Parkhurst with her Dalton Plan; and others all seemed to have based their ideas of individualization on this premise. So it was with the 24th Yearbook of the NSSE in 1923, *Adapting the Schools to Individual Differences*. In fact, until 1940 at least, this concept still seemed to control the thinking about individualization—if this can be judged by the 19th Yearbook of the NEA Department of Elementary School Principals, *Meeting Special Needs of the Individual Child*.

In the modern view of individualization, however, the process is thought of in much broader terms than merely an adjustment of the pace at which the individual child goes through a set amount of learning. As summarized by Frazier (*15*), individualized learning seems to have three unique dimensions. First, rather than being rate-oriented, it is seen as a multidimensional and complex matter. Instead of being conceived of as instruction in graded steps, individualized learning is seen to depend on insights obtained wherever possible. Thus, a kind of *mosaic* learning pattern is in evidence, one with an overlapping and circular rather than a rigidly linear or sequential pattern.

Second, it is felt that the extent to which traditional limits should be placed on what should be taught and on the learning expectations at the different grade levels is highly questionable. There are seen to be few, if any, limits put on individualized learning, in or out of school. Instead, learning is approached so that an easy transfer to learning outside the schoolroom is not only possible, but likely. This requires a broad concept of curriculum and instructional materials that range greatly in difficulty. Seeking for and self-selection of problems, and the arrival at creative rather than mechanical solutions, are demanded. The best example of the workings of the broad approach probably is reading. It is known, for example, that children who are taught to use reading in and out of school achieve in reading with significantly greater variability than they do in arithmetic, which is usually the most narrowly confined of all subjects to grade level expectations, and which, as ordinarily taught, allows little transfer to learning outside of school.

Third, individualized learning is believed to operate only with a great amount of child participation in planning the learning experience. It must be largely personal so that each child will learn what he needs to know. Achievement is expected at the child's level, therefore, and not at the standard for his age group. Accordingly, the child will occupy various roles in his school group and not continually be of the highest, middle, or lowest educational status.

The chief objective of individualized teaching, therefore, becomes the release of the potential in the individual learner. By human potential we mean everything with which the individual is capable of responding. It is the "total personal responsiveness without preconceptions concerning the limitations of that responsiveness" (*11*). With individual learning children are led to discover their potential powers and to deepen their understanding of themselves, and of others as well. As the individualized teacher demonstrates his concern over the potential he sees in individuals, they in turn learn to discover the potential of their fellows. In this way the route toward true humanitarianism is mapped.

It should be said at this point that there is little doubt that the implementation of such beliefs is not easy. There are pressures in the society that work against teaching the child as an individual. In his book, *The Organization Man,* William Whyte sees in today's society a climate which inhibits individual initiative and imagination, and the courage to exercise it against group opinion. It is not uncommon for the group, he says, to cling to some known disadvantage rather than risk the discomforture of change, or to seek group answers to problems that require individualistic, creative answers. In *Escape from Freedom,* Erich Fromm speaks of modern man's profound readiness to conform to common expectations and his profound fear of being different. Reisman sees him as bored, an escapist, and part of *The Lonely Crowd.*

Because of these and other pressures for conformity and against individualistic teaching, the teacher who would pursue this approach cannot be one who spends time complaining about the pressures of too much conformity. He knows it avails him little to protest about the forces set against individuality. He knows, too, there is no such thing as waiting for conditions to change so as to become favorable to individuality. These conditions he must make for himself. Individuality in teaching must crash through or perish, says Sylvia Ashton-Warner in *The Teacher,* the recounting of a remarkable plan of individualized reading used with New Zealand Maori children.

Consequently, to satisfy the rationale of individualized teaching the teacher must ask himself if he is willing to risk being thought of as an unusual, experimental teacher who takes chances, or "isn't it more comfortable to merge into the anonymity of the herd?" Furthermore, he must note for himself whether he dares to move away from the prescribed curriculum, the graded textbook, and whether he will be comfortable adjusting to a wide range of achievement. He must be willing to examine his ability to organize activities, and to bring the necessary friendship, security, and recognition to children so they will seek for self-development. Specifically, he must be able to develop problems whose answers can come from different levels of insight and other thinking abilities. He must resist the temptation to view subject matter coverage as the primary function of the school. He must have the confidence that he has the knowledge to teach reading without constant dependence on the teacher's manual of a graded textbook.

Translated into further terms of reading, these concepts of individualization accept and respect the fact that each child is an individual in his own right. It sees reading as a personal affair and thus assumes that instruction should be adjusted so as to bring out the individual's potential rather than to submerge it. In individualized reading the teacher is reminded constantly of the great motivating force of interest in learning. Olson's expression that normal children do not avoid learning but actively seek out appropriate learning activities is a statement on the force of interest. One can accordingly "trust the seeking behavior to tell us much about the readiness of a child for an experience" (30). Since it is dangerous to introduce basic frustrations into the life of the young child, it is best to let him select the time he is ready for reading and for different levels of books. The idea of pacing given by Olson refers to the acts on the part of the teacher which ensure that each child is provided with the materials that will motivate him to continue to strive when success is clearly within his grasp, and to avoid activities at a level clearly beyond his grasp.

A concrete illustration of how one group of teachers found these principles to be true in action was given more than a quarter of a century ago (39). To provide for individualization in reading these teachers tried dividing their classes into three or four groups of twelve to fifteen pupils each, and then divided each of these sub-groups again into two or three smaller groups. These groups then met for the supervised silent study of reading materials. Each group read materials of a different length and difficulty. After each study period each group had an opportunity to read orally to the other groups. These teachers, to their disappointment, reported that even with these nine or so smaller groups "it was found that not all children in a group could proceed at the same rate and that different children met different problems. Words readily recognized and retained by some were difficult for others. Consequently some children were held at too slow a pace with resulting habits of inattention and boredom, while others were forced beyond their powers and hence failed to master their own difficulties" (39:336).

In summary, the special value of individualized reading has been seen to be the especial respect for the child as an individual. It is believed his removal from an ability-grouping reading situation, that inevitably brings on feelings of superiority or invidious comparisons, also allows the teacher to help him better fulfill his special needs in reading. The child develops self-management in this process as he sees the true reasons for reading emerge, that is, reading for his own purposes. The teacher consequently is not required to follow prescriptions for teaching reading. Individualized reading recognizes that the teacher is able and can be trusted to teach reading properly. Teachers grow professionally, it is held, in proportion to the degree this recognition is given and as they become independent of the textbook. No longer have they to force children to meet predetermined standards. The need to invent motivation and independent activities closely tied to a prescribed text is banished. The child, normally curious and actively seeking of experiences consistent with his abilities, energies, and needs, will come naturally to reading if these conditions prevail. If given the opportunity he can make, with guidance, an appropriate selection of reading materials that fit his abilities and needs. He will pace himself at the rate at which he can most effectively exploit his potential, which ensures for him much successful experience in reading and little or no failure or need for remediation in the traditional sense. This success convinces him that the act of reading is a pleasurable thing, thereby creating further desirable attitudes. He realizes almost immediately that the true function of reading is that of solving problems, or of satisfying the need for pleasure in an individual and unrestrained manner. Consequently, freedom and the use of reading materials tend to be considered as synonymous, which is an important conclusion for any citizen of a democracy to realize.

Getting Ready for Individualized Reading

Since individualized reading demands of children an independence of effort and a certain degree of self-selection of reading materials it is obvious that this approach to reading will be very difficult to begin until the child has developed reading skills at such a level that he can read from available texts and trade books. It is helpful to remember, at this point, that some children do begin the first grade with the ability to read. Terman, in his early studies of gifted children, found that nearly half of those he studied had learned to read before starting to school. More recent evidence gathered by Dolores Durkin (*13*) would indicate that perhaps one per cent of all beginners have reading skills that range from 1.5 to 4.5 years of achievement. The expansion of the teaching of reading skills in the kindergarten, a movement lead by the experimentation of McKee and Lucile Harrison at Denver (*9*) will undoubtedly result in the development of reading abilities for some children in certain communities.

For the child who comes to school with no reading abilities, however, there must be, of course, an introduction to the reading process before he begins with the individualized approach. Any of the programs set up for typical children, described as basal reading, the language experience, the linguistic, or the phonetic approaches could serve this purpose. "Helping children to reach the stage of individual reading of their own self-selected books is a process no different from preparing children to join a reading group to attack their first pre-primer," is the advice of a first-grade teacher experienced in this problem (*38*).

In some instances the introduction of individualized reading can be made as the behavior of certain children in the reading group indicates they are gaining independence at the reader level, and thus can read from the basal text with little supervision from the teacher. It might be said, to certain children, "Lois and Stevie, since you seem to know the words in our book and don't need so much of my help, how would you like to find a comfortable place somewhere in the room and try reading to yourselves today, just you two taking turns reading to each other?" (*8*) Before long with this approach the teacher will find she can have an entire group reading aloud to each other in pairs or partners from different first-grade basal readers, but in different stories and at individual speeds. Soon some will begin to read completely by themselves. The teacher may want to sit in with this collection of individuals, at least close enough so that her help is available if needed. Other teachers have begun individualized teaching as soon in the first grade as a child finishes the first reader.

Ruth Robinson's plan (31) for introducing reading to beginners involved a pre-school conference for parents in the spring prior to their children's entrance to first grade. At this time demonstrations were given by teachers, with children, for these parents as to how to help their children learn to read a pre-primer supplied by the school during the summer before the children's entrance to first grade. This advice was simple: in five-minute periods, to begin with, tell your child each word, one at a time in the book, and have him repeat the word as he keeps his place. Parents were further encouraged to take their children to the public library for more pre-primers after the one supplied had been so read, and to exchange pre-primers with their neighbors who were going through the process. If it was not possible to schedule a pre-school demonstration for parents, teachers demonstrated the above techniques on the first day of school. The beginning formal instruction in first grade followed this same plan, that is, children were instructed to read aloud softly and individually from pre-primers as the teacher moved among them to give help as it was needed. More able children were used as helpers to fill in words for those who had difficulty going on alone. Often, helping children were seated next to children who occasionally needed help. By October, Miss Robinson reports, the average first grader in this program had read ten pre-primers. This simplistic procedure, combined with an early start with written composition used for additional reading material, brought on an easy transition to the individualized reading of trade books in the first grade.

Writing one's own beginning reading material instead of relying on basal readers is the heart of the so-called *language experience* preparation for individualized reading (25). In this plan for beginning first graders with formal language it is believed that anything a child can write (dictate to the teacher) he can read. In preparation for this dictation beginners in school share and discuss many experiences, and listen to and tell numerous stories. From this rich language experience they are led to conceptualize reading as speech written down. "The natural way for a child to understand what reading really is is to observe the recording of his own speech and the speech of others with the letters of the alphabet" (25:46). As the teacher takes dictation from the child she helps him discover the conventional written symbols that represent his speech. Lists of high frequency words, those of high interest, and picture dictionaries are all of help in this effort. Experience charts are constructed and read. Everything in the room is labeled. Pictures are drawn, labeled, and read. The dictated stories of the children are bound into "books," and thus become the primary reading materials of 'the first grade. From here the movement to self-selected reading of hard-cover texts and trade books readily follows. According to one teacher this may come thusly: "As all the language and first-hand experiences are going on, I begin to introduce simple books. I read each one to the children. They discuss it and dramatize it before it is put on the library shelf. The child must know what the book is about in order to tell whether he wants to go to it. The children begin gradually to gravitate toward these books, tell each other stories from the pictures, and begin to read the simple text" (*12*:98).

One of the best sources for detailed information on introducing individualized reading into the first grade is that given by Phylliss Adams (*1*). She suggests that in the spring of the school year first grade teachers attend an orientation meeting where individualized reading is explained. Then, during the last two weeks of the school year personal conferences should be held with each teacher. During these conferences reading bibliographies are provided so that during the summer vacation the teachers can become better acquainted with the information and research on the individualized program. At these conference times individual questions are discussed, and plans are made for procuring materials needed to carry out the program in the fall.

Dr. Adams has developed program guides for individualized reading based on the literature in the field (*1*). In these guides can be found (a) a definition of the approach; (b) principles on which it is based; (c) conditions essential for its success; (d) a detailed description of the necessary materials of instruction, both teacher-made, and pupil-teacher-made along with all the published materials; (e) ideas for grouping for skill development, for establishing routines and schedules, for preparing room environment, and for initiating the program; (f) and examples of pupils' and teachers' records needed in the evaluation of the readiness of children for the program and for their progress.

To develop the initial sight vocabulary necessary for individualized reading Dr. Adams believes there should be read many teacher-pupil chart stories, teacher-prepared news stories related to current classroom events, individually composed stories, and several pre-primers of the different basal reading series. She suggests the use of a list of core words taken from a variety of early reading materials.

The introduction of individualized reading can be accomplished, according to Dr. Adams, by either of two change-overs:

One-group-at-a-time change-over works like this: As soon as the teacher has appraised each child's stage of readiness, children with similar reading abilities are placed into groups. In most cases three groups are formed. Reading instruction is given in groups, although total class experiences are also provided through such an activity as developing experience charts. When a group has developed an initial sight vocabulary, has read one or more pre-primers, and is well under way in learning to read, they are allowed to engage in individualized reading—selecting their own reading material, and meeting for individual conferences with the teacher. The rest of the class continues to meet in groups for reading instruction. Gradually, as children participating in individualized reading are settled and making progress, a second reading group is disbanded and these pupils start on their way in individualized reading. This procedure continues until all children in the class are reading on an individualized basis (*1*:267).

Individualizing the reading program all at once with the entire class works in this way: The first few weeks are spent in getting acquainted, and carrying out the readiness program using published readiness materials as well as numerous class activities. At this time sight vocabulary is being developed through the reading of many group experience stories, individually dictated stories, and teacher-prepared news stories. When it is noted that several children (or even one child) have developed a small sight vocabulary, they are introduced to reading from a supply of varied pre-primers—fifteen to twenty-five or more—with each child selecting the book he wants to read. These children then meet individually with the teacher each day as well as engaging in the on-going group activities. As other children develop sight vocabularies they too meet individually with the teacher. This procedure continues until all children in the room are engaging in individualized reading (*1*:268-9).

Other less commonly used procedures might possibly be used to develop the reading skills needed to launch a child into individualized reading. One of these could be the use of the textfilm materials described by McCracken (*26*). With this material the initial reading instruction takes place at a projectional screen onto which the story from the basal reader is projected from filmstrips. All the children in the class, or groups of them, if one decided to modify McCracken's plan, carry on with the story in much the way it is customarily done with the basal reader. The advantage to this scheme, according to its originator, is that "Pupils in our primary grades are fascinated by the reading films. They call them 'movies.' Beginning classes often work vigorously and excitedly on one lesson, for nearly an hour at a time, with scarcely a glance away from the screen. For this reason, we consider 'interest' to be the principal value of the film reading method" (26:546).

Another plan for bringing children to a level of reading maturity necessary for individualized reading would be the approach as described in the writings of Bloomfield and Barnhart (5), McCracken and Walcott (27), and Daniels and Diack (10). These publications have in common what has been called the linguistic approach to reading instruction. Essentially this means that the first reading material for the child in first grade is made up solely of regularly-spelled words. The irregularly-spelled vowel and consonant sounds in words are then slowly and systematically introduced. A plan for combining this program and individualized reading would be to first take children through the regularly-spelled words. After this, for a time, they would read widely in easy-to-read materials in an individualized way. All the irregularly-spelled words would be given to them as needed. Finally, the irregularly-spelled words as presented in the linguistic materials would be slowly and systematically presented and studied at separate times with periodic opportunities for wide, extensive, and individualized reading to practice them, to increase comprehension and speed, and to allow each child to develop his reading ability at an individual pace.

Of these various procedures for introducing the child into the act of reading it can be seen that the language experience approach is most in keeping with the rationale of individualized teaching. Nevertheless, once the child has reached the point of the pre-primer or primer stage of word recognition, by whatever means, he is ready for individualized reading. At the level of the pre-primers in the basal reading series there have been introduced approximately 50 to 100 words. At the level of the primer this advances to a total of about 120 to 300 words, depending on the reading series that is used. There are now available many trade books that contain less than these numbers of total words in their stories. Also, it is increasingly easy to identify large numbers of trade books whose reading difficulty have been adjudged to be at the first grade level, or whose actual measured readabilities are at grade 2.5 or below.* It is at this point in the first grade, therefore, that the child is ready to enter into an individualized reading program regardless of which of the above procedures for developing this readiness the teacher has used. It is preferable, in the writer's opinion, to base an introduction into individualized reading on the ability to recognize a certain number of words rather than any other criterion—such as oral

---

*A comprehensive list of such books compiled by the writer is now available from NCTE, 506 S. Sixth Street, Champaign, Illinois.

reading speed, the number of "new" words per 100, results of readiness or mental tests, etc.

Organization and Materials

The content for the individualized reading program in the first grade as seen includes both texts and trade books, as well as stories and charts children write. These, along with any other writing of quality that can be found at the reading level of the children involved (20), provide the necessary materials of instruction. One essential difference from the ability-grouping, basal reader approach is that basal readers must take their place alongside trade books and other materials on the shelves and tables from which children choose them. The appeal of basal readers to the child is now on their own merit rather than as a prescription from a higher authority. While there is no pressure from the teacher on the child to select specific materials to read, the teacher does help guide the child to books on various topics so that his interests do not remain static. The teacher also judiciously protects the child from repeated frustrations with books over his head in reading difficulty. Most importantly, the teacher sets up procedures by which a child learns to skim books himself to see if they are beyond his reading abilities, or are of little interest to him. Some teachers group trade books alongside pre-primers, primers, and first and second readers on separate tables or shelves as an aid for the child in his selection. The child's responsibility at this point is to read his chosen book to its completion, and while so doing to plan a way to share it with his classmates.

In essence, after each child has chosen his book, an individualized reading period in the first grade would be conducted as follows: At the beginning of each session the teacher discusses with the group what their plans are for the period. Each child indicates his accepted responsibilities. Some children will indicate they will finish their book and plan for a way to share it. Lists of ways to share books are prominently displayed for assistance in this matter (12:46-53). Others may indicate they will read aloud with a partner, or will search for a new book. Some will need to complete a record sheet on their book to help the teacher keep an account of what they have read. The records of the books children read can be kept on graphs on which the child indicates how many books he has read under several categories. He can be led to make any number of comments about these books. Such a record can stimulate the child to refer to other categories of books in which he might be interested, or to see under how many categories he can read books.

After the children on individualized reading have turned to their announced activities, the teacher will call, as time allows, a selected number of them to read orally and to answer comprehension questions about the book they are reading. This assumes, of course, that the teacher has familiarized himself with the books the class has available for self-selection. During this conference he annotates in an ongoing record folder for each child the content the child has covered, what particular word recognition and comprehension problems he seems to have, what specifically and in general are his interests in reading, in what ways he shares his books and what corrective drill he needs. This form is best organized into a check list which allows for quick notations of these features of the child's reading, and which requires a minimum of writing. These conferences are of necessity very short in duration. The teacher thus can meet with six to eight children daily. After a few of these meetings with the individual child the perceptive teacher usually becomes aware of the child's shortcomings and can save time in the conference by anticipating them through questions and requests for certain reading responses. During the time of the individual conferences the atmosphere of the classroom is one of mutual helpfulness. Children help each other find readable books, or help out with an unfamiliar word. As with other approaches to reading instruction some children will require more of the teacher's time, as opposed to those who will be able to work independently with less frequent help and guidance.

At the end of the activity period the children usually join in a group to share with each other the books they are reading or have read. The teacher in this way gains further insight into their reading interests and reading abilities. Other impermanent groupings are made for special needs. For example, some children may be reading only a certain kind of book. The teacher can bring these together to introduce exciting books on other topics. At other times those who have shown a weakness in a certain word analysis skill may come together for practice on it. Sometimes it will be discovered that children have regressed in their social maturity and powers of self-direction. A session of supervised group activity would be called for. On occasion, because of interests in a single book, children will elect to read together the same material and join in a group to give their opinions and impressions of it. From common experiences with a story or book the group can plan dramatizations or art work such as murals.

Evaluation of the Program

The evaluation of individualized reading takes at least three general forms. First, the customary testing of reading achievement through the use of standardized tests is maintained. The growth of reading skills is also judged through observations of the individual's oral reading abilities in the individual conferences and as he shares his books in this way with others. His improvement in the skills of word recognition and analysis are seen as individual and group guidance is given in these matters. Beyond this, from the records the teacher and the child keep regarding the amount and kind of reading done, the teacher has a rather complete record of what the child reads. The variety of reading materials to which the child has been attracted indicates his various interests, of course. The third important aspect of the evaluation is the estimate of the child's reaction to reading. This is deduced largely by the degree of enthusiasm for the reading process he shows. The ways he manages his time, exerts self-control, and acts as a helpful aid to others in the class are other indications of his feelings in this respect. The extent of his initiative and creativity in sharing his reading with others, and the quality of his cooperation in these sharing activities give further evidence of his enjoyment and appreciation of reading.

In an overall sense the teacher judges the values and appropriateness of individualized reading, according to Lee and Allen, to the extent that:

1. productive thinking is generated,
2. freedom of expression is allowed,
3. individual talents and skills are used,
4. thinking is modified as new learnings are added,
5. curiosity is satisfied through exploration,
6. personal satisfaction is achieved (25).

Put another way, the individualized reading program is successful, says Jeannette Veatch, as:

1. large numbers and a wide variety of books are used,
2. children choose what they read,
3. motivation arises from children's interests,
4. instruction is on a one-to-one basis,
5. grouping is for a short term and for a specific, immediate purpose,
6. each reading lesson has elements of self-determination,
7. corrective work is integrated with other activities,
8. there are planned sharing periods,

9. only the best reading efforts of the child are checked,
10. gifted and slow learners progress at their own pace while one is not aggrandized and the other publicly stigmatized,
11. close personal interaction with the teacher serves the child's psychological needs,
12. reading at individual interest and ability levels fosters the development of skills,
13. skills are acquired as needed,
14. oral reading is a genuine audience situation, and as
15. reading becomes its own reward (37:12-13).

Research

As seen, the advocates of individualized reading make several claims for the approach as a superior one in beginning reading instruction. There can be found in the published literature several reports from those who have used the approach that agree with this premise. These are reports often substantiated by little more than an individual teacher's positive reaction to the procedure, however. These reports will not be discussed in detail here since the enthusiasm for individualized reading of such advocates may have biased their judgment. It is necessary therefore, to look for more substantial evidence as to the merits of the approach. One must ask, is there experimental data that can be used to compare the relative effectiveness of individualized reading and basal reader, ability-grouping practices in the first grade? Does this unorthodox procedure, in fact, bring on significantly greater amounts of reading achievement at this grade level?

There is a small number of studies that can be used to help answer these questions. The writer has located only a few investigations, of varying quality, that compared the individualized and the basal reader-ability grouping approaches in grade one. There are also a handful that were carried on with grade two pupils that have usefulness for this purpose.

In only one of these studies at the first grade level (6) was it found that basal reader-ability grouping brought on significantly greater gains in reading than did individualized reading. Here one class of first grade children was taught with the former approach for three months, and then were put under individualized reading for the next three months. The same teacher taught both experimental periods. During the three-months period with ability grouping the class gained seven months in reading achievement. With individualized reading they gained three months. It was noted by the investigator of this study, however, that usually growth in reading ability is greater in the first part of the school year with any method, than in the latter part, when individualized reading was used in this study. The differences in favor of ability-grouping were thought to be partially the result of this, therefore.

Four other studies found no significant differences between the reading growth of pupils under individualized reading and those under ability-grouping. Two of these, both doctoral studies, investigated an individualized versus a group teaching of word identification (23) and comprehension (7) to the same matched groups of sixty-eight first graders for seven months. Phylliss Adams (1) studied eighty-four pupils under individualized reading and eighty-eight under a basal reader-ability grouping approach for 102 days of teaching. She found no significant differences between the two groups except that the difference between the girls in the two groups was significant and favored the individualized reading group. This difference could be expected, however, since the girls in the individualized reading group had significantly higher reading readiness scores. The other investigation (32) compared the achievement of a class of superior first grade children with the two approaches.

Bliesmer and Yarborough compared the results obtained for 236 first grade pupils with the use of five different reading texts or materials that stressed the use of a "synthetic" approach to word recognition as versus the results gained for 248 pupils with five different texts or materials that stressed the "analytic" approach. They found that "a great preponderance of differences among means (ninety-two out of 125, 74 per cent) is found to be significantly in favor of the synthetic group." Among the five "analytic" approaches (of which individualized reading was one) there were found only six significant differences (out of fifty comparisons). These six significant differences all favored the individualized reading approach. These researchers concluded, "It would seem, therefore, that methodology, rather than specific programs or materials used, is the more decisive factor in the overall effectiveness of reading instruction in grade one" (4).

In a comparison of 365 pupils in an individualized reading program in the first grade with 343 in a basal program, the researchers of the Lakeshore, Wisconsin Curriculum Study Council found that the pupils in the individualized reading program were significantly superior to the pupils in the basal group in word knowledge, word discrimination, and in reading comprehension (24).

In two other studies it was found that individualized reading was superior to ability-grouping reading. Florence Sperry (35) identified first grade teachers as either oriented toward individualized reading or ability-grouping. She found the reading achievement in the individualized reading classes to be significantly higher than that in the ability-grouping classes. In a less extensive study (22), that compared one first grade under individualized reading with two under ability-grouping, it was found that the reading improvement of the former approach was the same as one ability-grouped class and two months above that of the other class. No test for the significance of the differences of these scores was made.

The few studies of individualized reading at the second-grade level tend to reflect the above findings. In his doctoral study Skolnick (33) found no significant differences between the reading achievement of six second-grade classes under individualized reading and six under ability grouping. Moreover, scores from the Anxiety Scale for Children revealed no significant difference between the reading achievement with the two approaches of high anxiety children (the top 25 per cent on the scale), and low anxiety children (the bottom 25 per cent on the scale). In a much smaller study (3) that compared eleven second graders under each of the two approaches there was found no significant difference in their reading achievement. Helen Field (14) in an early doctoral study also found that "extensive individual reading and class reading procedures are about equally effective in developing general reading ability in the second grade."

On the other hand, an older study by Laura Zirbes (40) found that in second grade extensive individual reading with short comprehension exercises was superior to class instruction for children who were reading more than sixty words a minute. Group instruction was found to be better for those below this rate. More recently, it was discovered (17) that significantly greater results in reading were obtained from the use of individualized reading in one second grade than in another. In a master's thesis (28) it was reported that four second grades under individualized reading made 1.4 years of reading gain compared to 1.1 years gain for four classes under ability grouping.

From this evidence the validity of the claim that individualized reading will bring on *greater* gains in reading than will ability-grouping does not seem to be substantiated. There can be little doubt, on the other hand, that the available evidence on approach has shown it to produce *as much* achievement in reading as does ability-grouping. Whether individualized reading develops better oral reading apparently has not been investigated.

The most pressing question for further investigation concerns the effects on the individual of the two approaches. It has been found (*19*) that by the middle grades over 80 per cent of children prefer individualized forms of reading over the basal reader-ability grouping forms. At this level children tended to prefer individualized reading for much the same reasons given by its teacher advocates. We need to find out if first grade children feel this same way about the two approaches, since there is some evidence that their interests are not reflected in basal readers (*34*). Would individualized reading with trade books give them greater satisfactions?

Further than this, investigations still need to be made as to whether the use of individualized reading does as it claims and makes first grade children more self-reliant and self-determining, more cooperative, more inventive and creative, more motivated for school work, and better psychologically adjusted to their teachers. Individualized reading is said to remove tensions from learning to read. As described above, however, Skolnick found no significant differences between the reading achievement of the children he studied with highest and lowest anxiety taught under individualized reading as versus ability grouping. In other words, children judged to have high anxiety achieved as well under ability grouping, a procedure believed by the advocates of individualized reading to create anxiety, as they did under individualized reading.

The differences in achievement between boys and girls in reading in general, need much more careful investigation. Specifically, it should be studied whether boys, who are believed to resist authority and regimentation more than do girls, achieve significantly better under individualized reading than under the more highly structured ability-grouping. Along with this the influence of the materials of ability-grouping as opposed to those of individualized reading need to be studied. Do children really respond best to highly organized material, tightly controlled as to its concepts and vocabulary? There is some evidence that one of the major claims of ability-grouping in the second grade—that it provides appropriate readiness—can be questioned (*21*).

The Future of Individualized Reading

The prognosis or expectation of success of individualized reading depends on many factors beyond even the rather extensive list above. The ability and personality of the teacher are of foremost importance, of course.

Where a certain teacher would have predictable success with ability-grouping, he could conceivably not do so with individualized reading, since here he must know enough about the techniques of teaching beginning reading without a continuous reference to the teacher's manual of a basal reader. As well, he must be familiar enough with children's literature to ask appropriate questions of children who have read various books, and to suggest ways they best can share them. The class he teaches also must be amenable to the processes of individualized reading. The approach takes self-direction and management, qualities which seem conspicuously lacking in some first grade classes. In addition to this the teacher of individualized reading must be a good manager of classroom time. He must know how to utilize small segments of time adroitly, and know how to establish time-saving routines if all the demands of the individualized reading program are to be satisfied.

The future success of the program is likely only if the teacher receives administrative support for his efforts. Above all, the school system must provide the extra books needed to make the approach feasible. This is demanding on many already strained school budgets. One administrator told the writer, off the record. "We believe in individualized reading, but frankly it is too expensive. We can't afford it." The recent report from the American Library Association to the effect that only about one-third of elementary schools have libraries provides little encouragement to begin an individualized reading program that is very demanding of books. Furthermore, there must be stimulation from administrators for teachers to use individualized reading. Specifically, this involves giving them an opportunity to see it in action, if possible. It means impressing upon them that administrators are knowledgeable about how the approach operates. Finally, it requires the school to provide teachers with the published materials on individualized reading, and with the book selection aids needed for choosing appropriate trade books for the first grade.

The final obstacle to the success of individualized reading is the unwillingness of some reading experts to admit that it is in fact a possible alternative approach to ability-grouping. These authorities insist there is not enough research evidence on the effectiveness of individualized reading for schools to undertake it. Paradoxically these are sometimes advocates of basal reader series which when introduced onto the book market were never tested against those already offered for sale, at the time or since. Actually, in the past twenty years there probably has been no general approach to reading that has been investigated more than has been individualized reading. Teachers who have reported their practice with the approach have denied the charges that opponents to it have made, namely, that it does not develop children's reading tastes or interests, that parents will not accept such a heterodoxical approach, that there is little or no possibility for group learning, that readiness is neglected, that children develop poor work habits, or that the reading related to curriculum studies is reduced and consequently study skills suffer. Too, some opponents of individualized reading insist that flexible grouping will adequately take care of individual differences. The very existence of flexible grouping in the ability-grouping approach is highly questionable, of course (*18*). While some of these allegations may have validity, a mere statement of them does not, as such, make them true, however. It does not aid the upward progress of reading instruction to make either claims or censure of individualized reading without evidence on which to base such statements. To this writer, in substance the evidence about individualized reading favors those who point to the number of studies in first grade and beyond that indicate that in comparison to ability-grouping it brings on equal reading growth in reading; who point to the numerous reports of improvement in the quality and quantity of reading with the approach; and finally who report the increase in children's personal commitments toward reading as a purposeful and pleasurable activity necessary for the full life. Under the proper conditions individualized reading should be used with no more fear of failure than with the ability-grouping approach.

REFERENCES

1. Adams, Phylliss S. *An Investigation of an Individualized Reading Program and a Modified Basal Reading Program in First Grade.* Ed. D. Dissertation, University of Denver, 1962, pp. 267-269.
2. ASCD Yearbook Committee, *Individualizing Instruction.* Washington, D.C.: Association for Supervision and Curriculum Development, 1964.
3. Baker, Julaine E. *A Modified Individualized Reading Program for Superior Second Grade Children.* Master's Thesis, Drake University, 1961.
4. Bliesmer, Emery and Betty H. Yarborough. "I. A Comparison of Ten Different Beginning Reading Programs in First Grade," *Phi Delta Kappan,* 47:500-504, June, 1965.
5. Bloomfield, Leonard and Clarence L. Barnhart. *Let's Read. A Linguistic Approach.* Detroit: Wayne State University, 1961.
6. Bohnhorst, Ben A. and Sophia Sellars. "Individualized Reading vs. Textbook Instruction," *Elementary English,* 36:185-190, March, 1959.

7. Braidford, Margaret. *A Comparison of Two Teaching Methods, Individual and Group, in the Teaching of Comprehension in Beginning Reading.* Ed. D. Dissertation, New York University, 1960.
8. Brogan, Peggy and Lorene K. Fox. *Helping Children Read.* New York: Holt, Rinehart and Winston, 1961, p. 29.
9. Brzeinski, Joseph E. "Reading in the Kindergarten," in *Teaching Young Children to Read* (Warren B. Cutts, editor), Washington, D.C.: U. S. Government Printing Office, 1964, pp. 20-58.
10. Daniels, J. C. and Hunter Diack. *Progress in Reading.* Nottingham, England: University of Nottingham, 1956.
11. DeHaan, Robert F. and Doll, Ronald C. "Individualization and Human Potential," in *Individualizing Instruction,* Washington, D.C.: Association for Supervision and Curriculum Development, 1964, pp. 9-28.
12. Draper, Marcella K., Louise H. Schwietert, and May Lazar. *A Practical Guide to Individualized Reading.* New York: Board of Education, 1960.
13. Durkin, Dolores. "Children Who Read before Grade I: A Second Study," *Elementary School Journal,* 44:143-148, December, 1963.
14. Field, Helen A. *Extensive Individual Reading Versus Class Reading.* New York: Teachers College, Columbia University, 1930.
15. Frazier, Alexander. "Needed: A New Vocabulary for Individual Differences," *Elementary School Journal,* 61:260-268, February, 1961.
16. Goodlad, John I. "Individual Differences and Vertical Organization of the School," in *Individualizing Instruction,* Chicago: National Society for the Study of Education, 1962, pp. 209-238.
17. Gordon, Ira J. and Clark, Christine H. "Experiment in Individualized Reading," *Childhood Education,* 38:112-113, November, 1961.
18. Groff, Patrick. "A Survey of Basal Reading Grouping Practices," *Reading Teacher,* 15:232-235, January, 1962.
19. Groff, Patrick. "Children's Opinions of Reading Textbooks versus Trade Books," Accepted for publication by *Reading Teacher.*
20. Groff, Patrick. "Materials for Individualized Reading," *Elementary English,* 38:1-7, January, 1961.
21. Groff, Patrick. "Readiness for Reading Vocabulary with Ability-Grouping," *Journal of Educational Research,* 58:140-141, November, 1964.
22. Hilson, Helen H. and Thomas, Glenn G. "Individualized Reading in First Grade," *Educational Leadership,* 16:319-322, February, 1959.
23. Izzo, Ruth K. *A Comparison of Two Teaching Methods, Individualized and Group, in the Teaching of Word Identification in Beginning Reading.* Ed. D. Dissertation, New York University, 1960.
24. Lakeshore, Wisconsin Curriculum Study Council. *A Three-Year Longitudinal Study Comparing Individualized and Basal Reading Programs at the Primary Level: An Interim Report.* Milwaukee: The Council, 1965.

25. Lee, Dorris M. and R. V. Allen. *Learning to Read Through Experience,* New York: Appleton-Century-Crofts, 1963.
26. McCracken, Glenn. "Reading Instruction for the Space Age," *Education,* 80:545-548, May, 1960.
27. McCracken, Glenn, and Charles C. Walcutt. *Basic Reading,* Lippincott, 1963.
28. McChristy, Antoinette. *A Comparative Study to Determine Whether Self-Selective Reading Can Be Successfully Used at the Second Grade.* Master's Thesis, University of Southern California, 1957.
29. NSSE Yearbook Committee, *Individualizing Instruction.* Chicago: National Society for the Study of Education, 1962.
30. Olson, Willard C. "Seeking, Self-Selection, and Pacing in the Use of Books by Children," in *Individualizing Your Reading Program* (Jeannette Veatch, editor), New York: Putnam, 1959, pp. 89-98.
31. Robinson, Ruth. *Why They Love to Learn.* Charlotte, N. C.: Heritage, 1960.
32. Roston, Sylvia W. *An Individualized Reading Program in a First and Second Grade.* Master's Thesis, National College of Education, 1962.
33. Skolnick, Sidney. *A Comparison of the Effects of Two Methods of Teaching Reading on the Reading Achievement of High and Low Anxiety Children.* Ph.D. Dissertation, University of Connecticut, 1963.
34. Smith, Ruth B. "Children's Reading Choices and Basic Reader Content," *Elementary English,* 29:202-209, March, 1962.
35. Sperry, Florence. *The Relationship between Reading and Achievement and Patterns of Reading Instruction in the Primary Grades.* Doctoral Dissertation, University of Southern California, 1961.
36. Tyler, Fred T. "Intraindividual Variability," in *Individualizing Instruction.* Chicago: National Society for the Study of Education, 1962, pp. 164-174.
37. Veatch, Jeannette. *Individualizing Your Reading Program.* New York: Putnam, 1959.
38. Vite, Irene. "A Primary Teacher's Experience," in *Individualizing Reading Practices* (Alice Miel, editor). New York: Bureau of Publications, Teachers College, Columbia University, 1958, pp. 18-43.
39. Webster, Elizabeth. "Individualizing Instruction in the Primary Grades," in *Meeting Special Needs of the Individual Child.* Editorial Committee of the Department of Elementary School Principals, NEA, Washington, D.C.: National Education Association, 1940, pp. 335-342.
40. Zirbes, Laura, et al. *Practice Exercises and Checks on Silent Reading in the Primary Grades.* New York: Columbia University, 1925.

WILLIAM D. SHELDON

SYRACUSE UNIVERSITY

3. Basal Reading Approaches

BASAL READING instruction is concerned with the development of those fundamental habits, attitudes and skills essential to effective silent and oral reading.

Rationale of the Program

The program rests on the assumption that a set of essential and fundamental skills are generally known and that these are of such a nature that a series of books, workbooks and manuals which present these skills in a sequential order are essential to their development.

Proponents of the use of basal readers suggest that an adequate basal reading program provides the essential prerequisites to successful growth in word comprehension, interpretation and all aspects of mature reading. However, it is recognized that the basic skills are brought to full use when children are lead to utilize these skills in reading of library books and the texts used in the various content areas.

Some basal reading experts suggest that the programs they have designed afford the springboard for successful application of reading skills in all of the life-long reading tasks of each individual.

The reading specialists who subscribed to Conant's *Learning to Read,* A Report of Conference of Reading Experts, supported the following statement:

> By and large, the child learns precisely what he is led to learn in response to the content and structure of the teaching materials. As applied to the teaching of reading, this means that effective teaching depends upon the careful programming of reading materials in terms of (a) the sound values of letters and letter combinations, (b) practice in recognition of words as wholes, (c) the apprehension of meaning both of single words and large units such as phrases, sentences, and paragraphs, and (d) the development

of suitable habits of adjusting one's approach to reading in the light of one's purpose for reading.

The rationale of the basal reading approach, as suggested by Chall (26) rests partly on research, partly on experience and partly on belief. The rationale has been and will be modified to adjust to new research and new experiences which lead to new beliefs about the most successful ways in which basal reading approaches can aid pupils to read most successfully.

Description of the Program

Method

The one word which seems most descriptive of basal reading approaches is eclectic. The procedures are eclectic in terms of the development of readiness, vocabulary, word recognition and word perception, comprehension skills and a love of literature.

The method of teaching involves certain common procedures which accompany each lesson. These procedures involve motivating children to read by various introductory devices, developing concepts basic to each lesson, teaching of certain word analysis skills, reviewing of known words and the development of an understanding of new meanings of these known words, introducing new words and their meanings, emphasizing the comprehension of what is to be read, what is read and what has been read.

Other aspects include the encouragement of critical thinking and developing a love of and taste for the best in reading material. At higher grade levels the basal program encourages the development of an ability to read the varied content material with understanding, the adjustment of rate of reading to purpose for reading, the mastery of such study skills as skimming, summarizing and reviewing and developing ability to use those locational skills which are necessary for all information seeking.

Teachers using basal readers ordinarily teach children in small groups and provide for acceleration or deceleration of the pace of instruction according to the individual child's ability to progress.

The method stresses continuity, sequence and integration and is most successful when these three basic ideas, first stated by W. S. Gray are supported by instructional practice.

Material

It hardly seems necessary to discuss the basal materials usually presented for first grade pupils but because of current misunderstandings we

shall present the various items in some detail. The material consists of
the following:

Several picture readiness books

Three or four preprimers, a primer and a first reader

Readiness tests, diagnostic in nature, are supplied before the preprimers
are used. These follow the use of readiness materials of a formal and informal nature. Some series include an achievement testing program with
tests designed to measure how well pupils master the program of vocabulary, word analysis and comprehension skills development presented at
each book level.

Every series has some sort of activity or workbook designed to provide
review or new material related to each story taught. At the first grade level
these workbooks are saturated with word attack and vocabulary review
exercises and limited comprehension lessons. While they are designed more
or less for independent use by pupils, many of the exercises require teacher
supervision.

A few programs have related filmstrips and recordings designed to give
practice in phonics.

Supplementary readers are also provided in some of the basal programs.
These are intended to give children practice in the new words they have
learned and to aid them to develop fluent silent reading in easy materials
based on a vocabulary already learned in the basal preprimers, primers
and first readers.

One such supplementary book is a hard covered preprimer which
reviews all the words and skills learned in the paperbacked preprimers.
Other supplementary books are either paperbacked or hard covered and
present known words and concepts in new story form.

The base of the program is the teachers manual or guide book. While
pupils do not use the manuals, they are actually the most important part
of any series. The manuals present the author's philosophy, a step-by-step
pattern of lessons, sources of supplementary materials, vocabulary lists,
diagnostic tests, and hundreds of ideas which teachers can use in developing additional word and comprehension building exercises.

At the present time most of the negative comments made about basal
readers focus on the preprimers and the limited content of these reading
materials. Many critics read a few lines from the first preprimer and evoke
laughter by clever parodies. Jokes related to the first grade teacher who
finds her car stuck in the snow or mud, or wedged between two other
cars, make the point. The teacher, allegedly brainwashed by the materials

used to teach first grade pupils, on seeing her car, shouts

"Oh, Oh, Oh,

Look, Look, Look,

Damn, Damn, Damn."

In our discussion of organization we will present some of the specific aspects of the content of basal readers.

The strength of the basal material lies in the careful development of vocabulary and word analysis skills in colorfully illustrated stories. The weakness of the material seems to be partly a lack of visibility in the way in which the vocabulary, word analysis, and comprehension skills are developed.

Organization

The basal reading program is organized horizontally and vertically. The horizontal organization involves the coordinated use of reader, workbook and manual and the correlated use of word cards, phonics charts, supplementary exercises presented in manuals, and other resource materials related to specific lessons.

An example of horizontal organization is taken from a first reader story, *Garden Spiders*. The story is presented in seven well illustrated pages near the middle of the first reader.

Prior to reading the story the teacher reads the manual and learns something about garden spiders. The manual offers suggestions related to the identification of probably known and possibly unknown concepts related to garden spiders and the story. It is suggested that pictures of spiders, bees, flies and caterpillars be presented and that a discussion of spiders, guided by certain questions, ensue.

Words previously presented and reappearing in *Garden Spiders,* with perhaps different meanings, are reviewed in context. New vocabulary is developed, both in context and in lessons developing phonic and structural analysis. Phrase reading exercises are presented.

The story is then read silently with key questions guiding this first reading. The illustrations are referred to when they lend to the meaning of the story.

After the story is read silently once, the children are directed to reread it in order to be able to tell the life story of the spider in sequence.

At this point the teacher can introduce two activity book lessons. The first lesson is done independently while the second is presented by the teacher. One of these is designed to develop the ability to recall and inter-

pret facts and ideas presented in the story. The other tests the visual
and auditory mastery of the forty-six words introduced in the unit in which
Garden Spiders appears.

Comprehension and vocabulary building exercises are recommended in
the manual which the teacher can present on the chalk board, through
discussion or on duplicated sheets.

Supplementary pages related to the story are found in prepared pads
and can be used to further strengthen word analysis skills, build comprehension and help firm up the study skills of outlining and summarization
related to this story.

Related to the introductory phonics lessons are certain examples presented in the phonics charts. The charts are used to pin-point the skills
of consonant substitution, rhyming endings, and the identification of vowel
sounds with written letters in words.

Enrichment activities are recommended which can either extend the
science background of the pupils or enrich their knowledge of geography
by a study of maps showing where spiders live.

Other enrichment type activities include reference to easy-to-read
stories of spiders found in other basal readers and in a variety of library
books. The teacher may read poems about spiders such as Howlitt's "The
Spider and the Fly" or A. P. Herbert's "The Spider." Recordings, films
and filmstrips which expand knowledge of the spider and his life are also
recommended in the manual, while filmstrips and recordings developing
the auditory-visual aspects of phonic development are also available.

It is this complex of concepts, word analysis skills, interesting silent
reading, comprehension development, discussion, and all the related
corollary activities that are overlooked by some critics and assumed to
be unnecessary by others. The aim in this horizontally enriched lesson
is to produce not only a person who knows words and how to analyze
them but to develop a clear appreciation of the rich offerings reading has
for him and the fact that reading is related to the broader aspects of life.

The vertical organization of basal readers, even at the first grade level,
would take chapters to describe. However, in brief, we can describe the
elements in the following four phases of vertical development:

1. Social organization
2. Vocabulary
3. Word analysis skills
4. Comprehension

Social Organization. The spiral of social organization is based on the home and the family. The immediate family life of one or two children is presented in readiness materials. Pictures depict the family in dozens of lifelike situations.

Preprimer story activities continue with the family and present a gradual broadening of activities beyond the home and into the school.

The primer centers its stories around the school, introduces pets, many new adults, the farm, and other special places, such as stores and the airport.

The first reader expands horizons by introducing children to the town or city at large with its helpers, zoos, rodeos, the library and again extends the characters to include a wide variety of individuals.

By the time the child has completed basal materials of the first grade he has increased the scope of his social interaction in ever widening circles, gradually increasing the distance traveled from home and his range of experiences and acquaintances.

Vocabulary. Vocabulary is introduced carefully and reviewed continuously. The new vocabulary is carefully controlled and presented according to the expert's consideration of the number of words which can be learned at a time by the average first grade child and the number of repetitions needed. The words presented are usually the high service words of the English language, and ordinarily word lists, supplemented by the special vocabulary needed in each story, supply the vocabulary. Studies have indicated that certain words are commonly presented in most basal programs while the need for certain words in particular causes the differences found in the vocabulary presented in the readers of different series. While there is a rather wide difference in the number of new words presented in various basal readers—and this difference may become greater because of new interest in increasing the vocabulary range of basal readers —the average number of words presented in preprimers is 60, in the primer 110 and the first reader 175. This number, of course, is smaller than the actual number of words learned by pupils in a grade one basal program, but there is no way of knowing how many words first grade pupils learn in addition to the 345 words which are mastered. An educated guess suggests that average pupils learn at least a thousand words if the 345 words taught directly are combined with words gradually acquired through analytic and contextual skills.

Word Analysis Skills. The leading basal programs present word analysis skills in chart form. One such chart suggests four general areas of word analysis skills presented in the grade one program: auditory discrimination, visual discrimination, and visual-auditory discrimination provided for phonic and structural analysis. The study of Mason (15) presenting the first grade analysis of a number of basal programs will be referred to under the section on research.

Briefly, at the readiness level, auditory discrimination is developed by:

1. recognizing and discriminating among common sounds, similar sounds, rhyming elements
2. recognizing the initial consonants
3. developing sensitivity to inflectional variants

Again, at the readiness level, visual discrimination is developed by a recognition of differences in configuration of:

1. forms and shapes of objects
2. letter forms
3. word forms
4. sentence forms

Incidentally the charge of configurationism leveled by a certain anti-basal reader group apparently does not consider the value of pre-reading visual discrimination training involving a variety of forms.

At the preprimer level pupils are taught a 60-70 word basic sight vocabulary through a visual and auditory discrimination of common sounds and forms, rhyming elements, initial consonants, and combine a knowledge of configuration clues, picture and context clues, and capital and lower-case letters with skill in recognizing inflectional endings added to nouns and verbs.

At the primer level the emphasis shifts from auditory and visual dis-crimination to visual-auditory discrimination which opens the way for intensive instruction in phonics and structural analysis based on a mastered vocabulary learned at the preprimer level.

During the primer lessons the visual discrimination clues learned previously are extended while certain aspects of phonic analysis, i.e. initial consonants, initial consonant substitutions and the rhyming elements are introduced and reviewed until a mastery level is achieved. Structural skills are reviewed and compound words are presented and studied.

The first reader lessons extend all the skills learned previously and add to the study of rhyming elements. Final consonants are studied and final consonant substitution is practiced while initial consonant blends are introduced and their substitution practiced. Initial consonant digraphs are developed. Added structural analysis skills include certain inflectional endings and the use of contractions.

'Some basal programs have included an emphasis on vowels at the first grade level while other programs develop the identification of vowels through their context in words. An emphasis on learning the alphabet and letter names has also developed recently even though several studies seem to indicate that most children enter the reading program with a rather broad knowledge of letter names, upper and lower case, and a sing-song, often nonsensical knowledge of the alphabet.

Comprehension. The sequence of comprehension skill development is harder to pinpoint than the more easily identifiable word analysis program. However, the following comprehension skills are developed almost simultaneously in the first grade basal reading program:

1. identifying the main idea
2. noting significant details and their relationships to one another and to the main ideas
3. making inferences and drawing logical conclusions
4. recognizing the motives, moods, and emotional reactions of story characters
5. recalling the sequence of story development
6. classifying related ideas and making generalizations
7. following directions

The subtlety with which comprehension skills are introduced in the manual lessons often leads casual observers to doubt whether or not such skills are actually developed at the first grade level at all. While developing tests of comprehension for pupils who had completed preprimers, primers and first readers, it was certainly apparent to the writer that while these comprehension skills are elusive and difficult to test, pupils could identify main ideas and important details, recall material in correct sequence, and follow directions. Less evident were skills related to 3, 4 and 6 above.

Current Status

Research Support for the Program in General

We cited Chall (26) above as stating that the principles of basal reading development were based partly on research, partly on theory, partly on experience, and partly on belief. It is evident that all four bases are questioned by the opponents of basal reading programs. While it has been particularly difficult to conduct research related to the efficacy of basal readers, there is a body of research related to various aspects of the basal reading program, either with or without a comparison to other approaches, which we cite below. The writer wishes, of course, that he had at hand the results of the present first grade study which should yield some definitive information related directly to the strengths and weaknesses of modern basal reading programs when compared to many other approaches to reading instruction in the first grade. But alas, these findings will not be available for at least six months and possibly not for several years.

Use of Basal Readers

Surveys conducted in the past by a variety of individuals, suggest the wide spread use of basal readers. It must be pointed out, however, that a 1965 survey is needed to determine whether the outpouring of other materials, phonics, linguistics, etc. and the introduction of language-experience approaches, individualized reading and the outcries of critics, have reduced the high percentage of users cited below.

Staiger (20), in a survey of 474 schools in 48 states found that 92 per cent of the schools surveyed used basal readers.

Stewart (22), in a survey of 107 city school systems, found that all used one or more basic reading series. Of these 87 per cent of the schools considered the skills program of the basic series to be adequate.

Belden (1), in a 1953 survey of the use of basal readers in New York State found that 95 per cent of the first grade teachers used basal readers for instruction. While a re-check of these schools is necessary, an informal sampling of some of the schools in 1964 revealed only slight changes in the use of readers. These changes were mostly a result of the adding of special phonics materials or the introduction of the Initial Teaching Alphabet. There was only a slight increase in individualized or personalized approaches found in this re-survey.

Vocabulary Control and the Content of Basal Readers

Vocabulary Control. The most vigorous attacks made on basal readers result, it seems, from vocabulary control and content. Critics argue that vocabulary control has made for dull, repetitious and uninteresting materials, while content is shallow, unrealistic and lacking in value in terms of style and literary significance.

Present research cannot answer the critics nor fully support the basal reader authors in terms of the wisdom of vocabulary control or the effect of the content on children.

Early (9), in discussing the reasons for vocabulary control, suggested that writers must choose words understood by their readers. Style will depend upon the choice of words and their order. Writers of preprimers can only be criticized for their use of restricted vocabulary when the words used distort what they have to say.

In the initial books of basal series the writer's purpose is to teach children to recognize words in print which have meaning in spoken form. Five- and six-year-olds know the meanings of thousands of spoken words but moving from speech to print is a formidable step, as most first grade teachers will testify. In fact, controls as they are now found in primary materials came as much from the reaction of teachers and pupils as from research studies.

In a study conducted at Ohio State University, first grade children indicated that they gauged reading difficulty in terms of vocabulary, text size, length of sentences and other aspects usually considered by the writers of basal reading materials.

Newton (16) has suggested that the basal primer may be deceptively difficult and suggests that we approach vocabulary revision in basal readers with thoughtful hesitancy.

As an example of the compact simplicity, yet complexity of our language, we refer to the 850 words of Basic English suggested by Richards and Ogden. Only 16 verbs and two auxiliary verbs are found on the list and twelve of them—*give, get, take, put, come, go, keep, let, make, say, see* and *send*—are fundamental to simple body action. When we ridicule the use of *come, go* and *see,* we poke fun at one-third of the basic verbs listed by Richards and Ogden.

The research of Gates (11), while not directly applicable to first grade readers, has certain implications concerning the effect of vocabulary control in first and second grade readers. It suggests that when pupils have had a careful reading program using basal readers they can analyze and recognize words at the third grade level far exceeding those they have been taught directly in grades one and two. Our previous comment—that while pupils are taught so many words directly in grade one they probably recognize three times as many by using their skills—seems to be somewhat supported by Gates' study.

Mason's (15) study of the word analysis program in eight widely used basal reading series and seven phonic series indicates the specific sequences of introduction of word recognition technique skills and understanding for the preprimer, primer and first reader levels of basal reading series. Any claim that basal readers depend on look-say as their only word recognition technique or do not have phonics instruction built into their programs is dispelled by this study. However, it is apparent that the differences in word recognition sequences are quite wide and that children who are taught in one series cannot switch to another and not suffer some loss of sequence in learning word analysis skills.

It is also observable in Figures 1-10 of Mason's study that basal programs extend their phonics programs through three years of instruction at least. A comparative study of phonics instruction in basal reading programs, as contrasted to phonics programs, must be carried on for at least three years, or until pupils complete the basal reader word recognition program, before valid comparisons can be made. Many of the phonics programs present the bulk of their word recognition skills, rules and generalizations in the first grade instructional program. Whether the skills remain is questionable.

It is said that the association of printed letters with their names is ignored in basal readers. This study reveals, for example, that one basal program provides instruction in naming all 26 letters, lower case and capitals, prior to the preprimer. Another program introduces the names of 11 letters in the readiness program, and with each word introduced in preprimer attention is called to names of first letters.

In the programs published by three companies the names and sounds of the letters are taught simultaneously.

All of the eight basal programs provide instruction in the alphabet and alphabetizing.

The phonics programs of three companies studied (13) are usually designed to be completed by grade one. Two go through the third grade while two are through sixth grade.

Most of the phonics programs start with association of phonemes with letters. One program teaches mnemonic devices for remembering the forms of letters before teaching names and sounds.

From the figures and tables presented by Mason it is obvious that the phonic programs are not similar in sequence, emphasis, or in the presentation of rules. The greatest similarity exists in the fact that phoneme-grapheme relationships are emphasized early in each program. (See pages 186, 187, 189, and 194-201 in Mason.)

In his well known study, Strickland (23) was particularly critical of the language patterns found in basal readers. Generalizations based on a sampling of basal reading books, not offered as conclusive evidence, suggest the following:

1. The basic subject, verb and object pattern was the only pattern to

appear in the samples of practically all books.

2. Patterns of sentences appeared to be introduced at random in a rather haphazard manner.

3. A pattern of structure, once introduced, seemed not to be followed by any sort of repetition or mastery.

4. There appeared to be no scheme for the development of critical sentence structure which paralleled the generally accepted scheme for the development of vocabulary control.

These questions were raised by the research:

1. Does the sentence structure in children's books influence the ease or difficulty of learning to read? To what extent?

2. Can a scheme of order in difficulty of language patterns be devised which can be utilized in textbook writing?

3. Can patterns of structure be introduced systematically and repeated until children learn them with ease?

Strickland's pursuit of the answers to these questions and the finding of them might well lead to some revolutionary steps in the writing of children's readers.

Content

Criticism of the content of basal readers reached the New Yorker readership when in a recent cartoon a large moronic looking football player was depicted seated on the bench saying, "Jim has the ball. Jim can run. Run Jim Run." This, like the teacher joke, sums up to a certain extent the general attack on basal readers and their content. It suggests that the critics have read the first preprimers and have based their negative reactions on a survey which takes them no further than page 26 in this first reading book.

Research on the content of basal readers is limited. Most of the research is of the counting sort performed by a number of master's and doctoral students. By and large useful, critical evaluations are lacking, and we learn only what was apparent through reading readers and counting items.

One of the better studies of content is that of Lorenz (14). She found that the characters in first grade readers lead a healthy, happy life. They were gentle and considerate in their dealings with others. Children and parents alike dressed in a conservative style. Homes and neighborhoods were tidy and attractive.

The children were occasionally playfully mischievous but never more than that. Basic family activities were engaged in as far as play and recreation were concerned. About 85 per cent of all activities were related to recreation, home duties, and educational and pleasure trips.

There were no vices, illnesses, or other negative aspects of life depicted. In summary Lorenz found that basal readers offered families of flawless health and personality and nothing of a controversial nature.

Wargny (24), compared the content of basal reading series and the story content in the McGuffey readers. He found a white middle-class culture presented in the readers and that the McGuffeys portrayed a more realistic picture of the world. Wargny raised certain questions as a result of his studies:

1. What is the place of the multi-racial texts?
2. Is there a need for portrayal of socially unacceptable behavior?
3. Should sorrow and unrestrained emotion be evidenced?
4. Should birth, death, mourning, divorce, working mothers, poverty, migrant workers, rejection by parents, hostility be shown?

These are questions which, like those related to the general place of realism in children's literature, need answers in research and in usage.

Byers (4) explored the interests of first grade pupils and discovered that the topics of greatest interest were science and nature, possessions, personal experiences, family and home activities, and outdoor recreation. In analyzing the content of first grade readers, it was suggested that readers should continue to develop the familiar and near at hand, but place more emphasis on science.

Rogers and Robinson (17) in a recent study sought an answer as to what first grade children wanted to read. The study included three hypotheses and related conclusions:

Hypothesis One. First grade children want books which will enrich their knowledge with the world in general, rather than books limited to relating stories about familiar daily activities of children like themselves.

This hypothesis was partially rejected. The children were interested in make-believe, happiness, humor, adventure, history, family, anxiety and today's world, in that order.

Hypothesis Two. Boys have markedly different interests than girls. This hypothesis was partially supported. Boys were more interested in adventure and history than girls, less interested in the family. Girls were more interested in family, home life and romance than boys.

Hypothesis Three. Poor readers had the same interests as good readers. This was supported since good and poor readers had similar interests.

An important question was raised about this research by the writers.

They asked whether or not the school program had already influenced interests so that the interests expressed were those of the existing program and therefore imposed on the pupils, rather than the interests they might have expressed if they had not had their opinions influenced by school experiences.

Williams (25) investigated the opportunity for developing critical reading through basal readers. All the series examined provided some exercises and direction for the development of fundamental reasoning abilities required for active critical thinking.

Other Research

Carterette and Jones (5) applied a redundancy measure to two series of graded readers and found that basal books at the first grade level were more redundant than level one materials in children's free-reading choices. The findings suggested to the authors that these basic readers may be too redundant to be interesting. The mean word length is similar in the two basal series and increases from level to level, whereas, in free reading choices it does not change systematically, being high even at level one.

The authors indicate that the greater mean word length for free choices at level one inclined them to believe that there may be an undesirable restriction in word length in basic readers.

The authors found that long and unusual words, if used repeatedly, produced easy reading. The point of importance suggested to the authors is that a small vocabulary can be used without restricting it to words of greatest frequency in the language—a practice, say the authors, yielding dull stories.

Mean sentence length, although similar in the two series, is far shorter than in the free-reading choices. The restriction in sentence length implies a restriction in grammatical forms.

In conclusion the authors state that basic readers have a constrained syntax, reflected in short sentence length, which is neither congenial with, nor typical of, natural spoken language. They conjecture that the lack of congruence between spoken and written language may well be one of the factors contributing to difficulty in learning to read.

Research in Progress

The most important research that is now being conducted relates to the first grade study sponsored by the United States Office of Education. Some

27 centers are conducting studies of methods and materials used in the first grade. Basal readers are being compared with linguistic materials, various phonics series, ITA materials and the like.

No conclusions will be available from this study until 1966. However, a preliminary report made by the research team at Syracuse University, where basal readers, linguistic materials and a phonics series are being used, indicates that after six months of instruction, good readers are learning rapidly in all three procedures while poor readers seem to have greatest difficulty with the non-basal materials. However, any judgment concerning the effect of the three approaches must be viewed as premature until the experiment ends and the data are analyzed.

Many other studies are underway related to first grade reading. These include inquiries into content for boys, the effect of listening-viewing materials on slower readers, the use of words in color, the development of predictive devices to alert teachers to poor readers, and a variety of tryouts of linguistic approaches to first grade reading.

Without doubt the research eliciting the most response to interest is that related to ITA and carried on in Syracuse, Chicago, Hofstra, Bethlehem and in Great Britain.

The Future of First Grade Basal Reading Programs

It is fairly apparent that changes are already taking place in basal readers and that other changes will take place during the next few years.

The first changes have to do with the provision for able kindergarten children. It seems apparent that in spite of all protests publishers will prepare basal materials for the kindergarten. These will undoubtedly contain not only the content of picture readiness books but also exercises on letter names and sounds, phonics lessons, and the development of a sight vocabulary of considerable proportion.

The phonics program in basal readers will undoubtedly become more visible and the exercises will be pushed down from second to first grade. Basal phonics programs, for good or bad, will resemble those now present in several of the more frequently used phonics programs.

Basal readers will be multi-racial and urban centered. This trend is already apparent and will soon include all basal reader programs.

Story content will be more mature and the controlled vocabulary will become so large as to more or less abolish the concept of vocabulary control altogether. The content will be more science oriented and special attempts will be made to increase the story and illustration appeal for boys.

The results from the first grade study will determine to a limited extent the place of ITA, diacritical markings, linguistic approaches, and language experience and individualized reading.

It is apparent that writing and reading will be taught simultaneously or perhaps that writing will precede reading.

Some of the changes suggested above have taken place, the rest seem inevitable. It must be remembered, however, that lasting changes from the present program will only take place as the changes are demonstrated to be effective with boys and girls.

It would be amusing to predict the present and immediate future changes which will and will not last, but we will refrain from this particular bit of guessing or speculation.

REFERENCES

1. Belden, Bernard R. "A Study of Selected Practices Reported in the Teaching of Reading in the Kindergarten and Primary Grades in New York State." Unpublished doctoral dissertation. Syracuse University, 1955.
2. Brown, Charles M. "Whether Basal Reading?" *Education,* 82:3-5, September 1961.
3. Bureau of Applied Social Research "Reading Instruction in the U. S." A preliminary report. Columbia University, 1961.
4. Byers, Loretta. "The Interests of Space-Age First-Graders," *Elementary School Journal,* February 1964, 64:237-241.
5. Carterette, Edward C., and Jones, M. H. "Statistical Comparison of Two Series of Graded Readers," *American Education Research Journal,* January 1965, pp. 13-17.
6. Cleland, D. L., and Miller, A. B. "Instruction in Phonics and Success in Beginning Reading," *The Elementary School Journal,* February 1965, pp. 278-282.
7. Conant, James B. *Learning to Read,* A Report of a Conference of Reading Experts. Princeton, N. J.: Educational Testing Service, 1962.
8. Dayton, Benjamin, and Alice Burton. "The Basal Reader in the First Grade," *Elementary English,* April 1955, pp. 237-239.
9. Early, Margaret J. "Is Vocabulary a Basis for Selecting Books?" *The Instructor,* November 1963, pp. 70-76.
10. Felton, Wilma. "The Values of Workbooks in a First Grade Reading Program," *Elementary English,* October 1957, pp. 377-382.
11. Gates, A. L. "Vocabulary Control in Basal Reading Material," *The Reading Teacher,* November 1961, pp. 81-85.

12. Herrick, V. E., Anderson, D., and Pierstorff, L. "Basal Instructional Materials in Reading," *Development in and Through Reading,* NSSE Chicago, 60th Yearbook, pp. 165-188.
13. Hymes, James L., Jr. *An Evaluation of Basic Readers for the School Beginner,* Row Peterson & Co. (Advertising).
14. Lorenz, E. "A Comparison of Family Life, as Depicted in Primary Readers With the Structure, Activity and Environment of Average American Life." Unpublished master's thesis, Iowa State Teachers College, August 1958.
15. Mason, George E. "An Analysis and Comparison of Programs for Teaching Word Recognition in Basal Series and Phonics Materials." Unpublished doctoral dissertation, Syracuse University School of Education, June 1963.
16. Newton, Eunice Shaed. "The Basal Primer May be Deceptively Easy." *Elementary English,* March 1963, pp. 273, 274 and 334.
17. Rogers, Helen, and Robinson, H. Alan. "Reading Interests of First Graders," *Elementary English,* November 1963, 40:707-11.
18. Sheldon, W. D. "What Research Says About Vocabulary Control and the Content of Basal Readers," *Children Can Learn to Read, But How?* Coleman Morrison, Ed. Rhode Island College Reading Conference Proceedings, 1964, pp. 70-77.
19. Spache, George. *Reading in the Elementary School.* Boston: Allyn and Bacon, Inc., 1964, p. 356.
20. Staiger, R. C. "How are Basal Readers Used?" *Elementary English,* 35:46-49, January 1958.
21. Stauffer, Russell G. "Breaking the Basal Reader Lockstep," *The Elementary School Journal,* February 1961, pp. 269-276.
22. Stewart, David K. "Values and Limitations of Basal Readers," *Materials for Reading,* Helen M. Robinson, Ed. Chicago: University of Chicago Press, 1957.
23. Strickland, Ruth G. *The Language of Elementary School Children: Its Relationship to the Language of Reading Textbooks and the Quality of Reading of Selected Children.* Bulletin of the School of Education, Indiana University, Vol. 38, No. 4, July 1962.
24. Wargny, Frank O. "The Good Life in Modern Readers," *The Reading Teacher,* November 1963, 17:88-93.
25. Williams, Gertrude. "Provisions for Critical Reading in Basic Readers," *Elementary English,* May 1959, pp. 323-331.
26. Chall, Jeanne. "Innovations in Beginning Reading," *The Instructor,* March 1965, p. 67.

CHARLES C. FRIES

EMERITUS, UNIVERSITY OF MICHIGAN

4. Linguistic Approaches to First Grade Reading Programs

O N THE WHOLE linguists have produced very few materials for actual series of reading texts from which to teach beginning reading.

Linguistic Approaches

Robert A. Hall, Jr. *Sound and Spelling in English,* Chilton Co., Philadelphia and New York, 1961.

Frances Adkins Hall [Series of developmental readers], *Linguistica,* Ithaca, N. Y. 1956.

Henry Lee Smith, Jr. and Clara G. Stratemeyer. *The Linguistic-Science Readers, A Basic Reading Program,* 1955. Now expanded by Jack E. Richardson and Bernard J. Weiss and published as *The Linguistic Readers* by Harper and Row, Publishers, Evanston, Ill., 1965.

Leonard Bloomfield and Clarence L. Barnhart. *Let's Read, A Linguistic Approach,* Wayne State University Press, 1961.

Ralph F. Robinett, Pauline Rojas, and Staff. *Miami Linguistic Readers.* Ford Foundation Project, Dade County Public Schools Board of Public Instruction, Miami, Florida, 1964. (The Miami Linguistic Reader Series is designed to help teach beginning reading to pupils whose preschool language was other than English.)

Charles C. Fries, Agnes C. Fries, Rosemary G. Wilson, and Mildred K. Rudolph. *A basic reading series developed upon linguistic principles.* Eight Readers, Eight Practice Books, A Manual and Guide entitled To Teach Reading: The Transfer Stage, and a book for teaching the letters of the English alphabet.

Special Meanings of the Words We Use

1. The term *linguistic* in our discussion here must be clearly separated from its popular use in English as meaning "anything and/or everything that has to do with language."

2. The term *linguist* here must also be clearly separated from its popular use in English as meaning anyone who can speak one or more foreign languages.

3. *Linguistics,* as used here, means the *body of knowledge and understanding concerning the nature and functioning of human language* achieved by the scientific study of the structure, the operation, and the history of a wide range of very diverse human languages. (This body of knowledge and understanding has been called "linguistic science," "sprachwissenschaft," for more than a hundred years.)

4. A *linguist* as used here is one who is a specialist in this body of knowledge and understanding—one who, by *profession,* teaches it and/or, by research, contributes to its advancement. (A *linguist* is one who *knows about* the structure, forms, and operation of a great many languages, although he may not have developed the special habits necessary to **use** any of those languages in conversation.)

A *linguist,* then, is one whose special field of scholarship is linguistic science. *Linguistic science* is here understood to be a body of knowledge and understanding concerning the nature and functioning of human language, built up out of information about the structure, the operation, and the history of a wide range of very diverse human languages by means of those techniques and procedures that have proved most successful in establishing verifiable generalizations concerning relationships among linguistic phenomena.

In this much loaded and difficult definition there are five essential features that cannot be separated, for each succeeding feature is a qualifier of what has preceded. Perhaps the following arrangement of the parts of this definition may serve to give these important features their relative prominence.

Linguistic science is

(a) *a body of knowledge and understanding,*

(b) (knowledge and understanding) concerning the *nature and functioning of human language,*

(c) (this knowledge and understanding) built up out of *information* about the *structure,* the *operation,* and the *history* of a *wide range of very diverse human languages,*

(d) (this knowledge and understanding built up) *by* means of those *techniques and procedures* that have proved *most successful* in *establishing verifiable generalizations,*

(e) (verifiable generalizations) concerning *relationships among linguistic phenomena.*

5. By *linguistic approach* to a first grade reading program we mean here a body of materials designed to teach beginning reading which

a. is definitely selected and arranged according to the principles and assumptions of language learning derived from the body of knowledge and understanding indicated above as the substance of linguistics (linguistic science);

b. is taught by methods, procedures and practices which are in harmony with this knowledge and understanding, and, in which conflicting methods and conflicting habit-forming pupil exercises are rejected.

6. The linguist's *professional field of competence* is the body of knowledge and understanding concerning the nature and functioning of human language. To apply that knowledge and understanding to the problems of effective "doing" in any sector of human activity, the linguist needs another competence in the "engineering" aspects of that application.

In similar fashion, the professional field of competence for specialists in psychology or in reading is not "linguistic science." To deal with problems that concern the nature and functioning of human language such specialists also need a second competence in the field of linguistics.

The Linguistic Nature of the Reading Process

The usual child of five has learned to talk. We are not concerned here with those who do not talk well enough to get along in their community. They constitute a different kind of problem.

The actual control of his native language by the five-year-old child is much more complete than persons other than linguists have assumed. From the point of view of a reading program we are concerned primarily with what the child *understands* as it is said *to* him, not what he himself says. His receptive language control is much greater than his productive language control. The basic question concerning his language becomes the following. "Just how much meaning and what meanings does the child receive or recognize when his parents, his teachers, his companions talk to him? If you read to him or tell him a simple narrative about going to a familiar store to get a ball, just what will he understand?" A five-year-old child will get some meanings from that "talk." The basic question for his reading becomes the following. "Just what must that five-year-old child learn to do now in order to get, by means of his own reading, the *same meanings* that he can get when he hears it? When he can get from his own reading the same meanings he can get from your telling him, he can *read* up to his language ability of that time. From our linguistic point of view a person can read in so far as he can get from special sequences of graphic symbols on a printed page the same fullness of meaning that he gets when these meanings are told to him in talk.

The process of learning to do reading, is the process of learning to transfer the already achieved ability to get meanings from talk in a time sequence to a new ability to get the same meanings from seeing representations of this same talk in a direction sequence on a surface. His reading progress and achievement is most realistically measured with his receptive language achievement as the base.

Learning to read is not learning to *know* something, it is learning to *do* something. No amount of knowledge about a language, however great, will, of itself, enable one to speak that language.

The materials and methods here set forth assume as their primary objective *not knowledge about reading but ability to do reading.* They aim at a step-by-step building of specific habits and abilities that lead directly to independent reading on the part of the pupils—*independent reading with a feeling of security in what they are doing.*

Learning to read must begin with and build upon the language control already achieved by the pupils. The reading must at every step be tied to the language of the child. Word recognition means a recognizing of the "word" as it appears spelled in letters as the same "word" that the child knows in his "talk." It is a recognition of an old friend now appearing in a mask—one whose "tone of voice" is recognized well.

The beginning steps in reading must all have this same fundamental character—the "words" as they appear in the spelling, and the "sentences" in which the "words" are joined together must all be recognized by the pupils as familiar, although somewhat masked, parts of the language they use every day. The first stage of learning to read consists of a building up by the pupils of the habits of identifying the "words," in their spelling-pattern dress, as the same words as those they know very well when they hear them in talk.

It is assumed that much of the school time outside the "reading period" itself will be given to the stimulating of "talk" by the children, for the sake of having them grow both in the vividness with which they can react to their experiences, and also in the fullness with which they can communicate those reactions. But the materials, *of the reading period itself*, in the "transfer" stage of the child's growth can be most effective by being adequately controlled. Within this control there is plenty of room for well-formed sentences in *coherent sequences*. A very few words, which the child knows orally, are presented as fitting into one of the types or matrixes of a pattern, and then immediately practiced by being read in sentences that belong to a sequence. There is no learning of lists of words at any time. The precise, rigorous controls of selection and sequence are embedded in the reading materials and not easily apparent in a hurried or superficial examination.

The most important first step in *preparing to learn to read* is the building up of high speed recognition responses to the letters used for the printing of English. It is true that adults who have learned to read well are usually not conscious of the separate letters of the words as they read. This fact, however, does not furnish any basis for concluding that the pupil at the beginning stage can learn to read by ignoring the special sequences of the letters that identify the separate words. He must master the whole set of letters by learning to recognize the special shape that identifies each letter and separates it from all other letters.

The instant recognition of individual letters as they stand alone is, however, not enough. Letters must be recognized as they appear in sequences. The order of the letters in the directional sequence of left to right acts as a fundamental marker for the discrimination of lexical units. The significant means of the identification and the discrimination of words in print are not only the different letter units that compose the sequence unit but also the order within that unit always seen from the single point of view established by English writing.

The Linguistic Significance of Present-day English Spelling

English spelling changed drastically during the period between the death of Chaucer in 1400 and the birth of Shakespeare in 1564. This changed character of English spelling is revealed in the vigorous arguments in the middle of the 16th century concerning the deviation from "reasonableness," and in the measures devised for bringing it back to its "due order and reason," "howe to write or paint the image of mannes voice most like to the life or nature." "The vices and faultes of our writing" were listed and condemned—"the use of the same letter for many sounds," "the use of many letters for the same sound," the "abuse" of "some letters to put a difference betwixt . . . wordes of one sound," "the superfluity of letters in writing," and to "shew the derivation and spring of some wordes borrowed or taken forth of strange tongues."

The new feature of this change was the fact that the *old spellings remained as patterns* and now represented the new pronunciations. This continuation of the use of the old spellings to represent the vowel phonemes, as now changed by the shift, put Modern English spelling out of line with the use made of the "Roman" alphabet by other languages. It even put it out of line with the English use of that alphabet during the Old English and the Middle English periods. By the end of the 16th century English spelling had accepted and extended for part of the vocabulary the "etymological" principle and, with it, the use of letters "silent to the ear" but "eloquent to the eye."

A new principle of representation became dominant. The spelling-patterns that developed historically pulled exceptions into conformity. The actual basis of the representation of the vowel phonemes changed from *items* of graphemes to *patterns* of graphemes.

The spelling-pattern approach used here, to a superficial examination, may seem to show features quite similar to those of a variety of the other approaches and "methods" that have been used in teaching beginning reading. However, this spelling-pattern approach is, in fundamental principle, quite different from any of them.

This spelling-pattern approach does explore and use the relation between the language as heard and spoken and the language as read and written. It is not, however, any of the *phonic* methods commonly discussed, nor is it any of the so-called *phonetic* approaches. It does not seek and emphasize correspondences of individual letter-individual sound. It does give attention to whole words rather than to isolated sounds but it is not any of the well-known "word" methods. At the beginning it uses a considerable proportion of the so-called "three letter words with short vowels" but it is not the "word family" approach.

One major special characteristic of this spelling-pattern approach is the fact that the attention is not centered upon the learning of individual words; nor is success measured by the number of the words the child has learned to recognize. For such a learning of individual words it is essential that these particular words themselves be repeated over and over, and it is only the word itself that is learned. On the contrary, in the spelling-pattern approach it is the pattern itself that is repeated frequently, using a variety of different words and matrixes. The response to the spelling-pattern through different words is made so frequently that that response becomes a fixed habit. With such habits of responses to the patterns and the matrixes, the pupil can be led to make instant extensions of recognition to other individual words in the same pattern and to read words of his receptive vocabulary that he has never seen written before.

The separate spelling-patterns are enforced by constant repetition in minimum contrast with other spelling-patterns. The objective is the building up of habits of rapid recognition responses, not only to contrastive items in a pattern, but to contrastive items in a system of contrastive patterns.

The spelling-pattern approach takes maximum advantage of all the *regularities* that the orthography of English has developed throughout the history of English writing. The patterns of Modern English spelling are primarily those that arose during the Early Modern English Period, i.e. from the beginning of printing in England to the latter part of the seventeenth century. In the spelling-pattern approach the criteria for identifying the separate words are not vague and general shapes but precise and sharp—the criteria of the language itself. The major and the minor sets of spelling-patterns include all but a very few English words.

By the end of the first 325 pages of our reading materials the pupils have become familiar with sets of words that exemplify most of the matrixes or types of spelling-patterns that make up what has been called here "the first major set of spelling-patterns." By this time the pupils will have, therefore, not only learned to recognize rapidly the particular 523 words that they have used in their readers but also will have developed the habits of recognizing rapidly any and all words of their receptive vocabulary that in the context of their reading, fit the various spelling-patterns of the first major set. Pupils are therefore able to read many words that they have never seen written before. Developing this ability from the beginning is one of the chief objectives of the spelling-pattern approach.

Reading for Meanings

From the very beginning, reading is developed as a means of acquiring meanings—not only the meanings of the separate words, but also the grammatical meanings that attach to structures in sentences, and the cumulative meanings of sequences of sentences in connected discourse.

The approach here assumes that language is man's chief device for storing and sharing meanings. With the invention of writing, the storehouse of man's knowledge has attained enormous capacity. Reading is the only key to that immense storehouse. The "words" as written have meaning for us only as these written "words" are connected with the "words" of our spoken language. But the isolated word alone can be used in so many situations that only as these "words" appear in the grammatical patterns that make sentences, do they actually convey precise meanings.

It is not, however, isolated sentences that convey the most important meanings we share, but rather sentences in sequence with the cumulative meanings of connected discourse. This series, therefore, begins the reading not with lists of words to be pronounced, but with three "words" to be recognized and at once used in three or four sentences with consecutive meaning.

The three basic words all fit a single type of spelling-pattern.

cat	Nat is a cat.
Nat	Is Nat fat?
fat	Nat is fat.
	Nat is a fat cat.

The "reading" thus begins with such a sequence as the following, using in addition to the three patterned words the familiar word *is* and the phrase *a cat*.

The significant elements of the meanings here are "words" in sentences which are joined in a sequence. All these elements of meanings are in the language forms that the pupil already knows. The reading process which the pupil is learning is the recognizing of the written forms in their directional sequence as standing for the "words," "sentences," and "sequences of sentences," the meanings of which he already knows and uses.

All the words that are introduced are thus not only immediately put into sentences, each one of which has a meaning, but the three sentences in sequence have cumulative meaning which is summarized in a fourth one. For the series, the very first book given the pupil (equal to the usual first and second preprimer), therefore, contains only some forty words; but these forty words are used in more than two hundred and sixty sentences through which the use of reading for meanings is developed from the very opening lesson.

These more than two hundred and sixty sentences appear, *not* as separate unconnected sentences, but in some fifty sequences or units of three or more sentences each.

Real reading is "productive reading." It is not only an active responding to all the signals of meaning represented in the writing, but also the carrying forward and building up of such a complete understanding of the sentences in sequence as will make it possible to fill in the patterns of tone, the special stresses, and the pauses of grouping that the live language of speech uses. Real reading is never a *passive* process of receiving meaning and saying words.

In order to make sure that pupils move easily into this sort of "productive reading," without having to correct interfering habits, attention to "expression" begins immediately. "Reading with expression" means nothing more than using in oral reading the intonation sequences (the sequences of musical pitch or tone) that characterize the ordinary talk of English speakers.

Normal English speech is not in a monotone. These variations of tone in the sequence of speech, however, are not haphazard and lawless. "Reading with expression" is more than avoiding a monotone. The sequence of tone in normal English speech follows certain major patterns within which there is considerable individual variation. It is essential that these major patterns of tone sequence be followed in oral reading by the teacher and by the pupil from the very beginning.

Using the major patterns of English intonation is *not* for the pupil (or for the teacher) learning to do anything new. As a matter of fact, fitting into the tone patterns of the intonation sequences of English is perhaps the very first thing the child learns of the language. Most normal children of six speak their language using all the intonation patterns of their linguistic community.

We do not aim to teach the pupils the facts concerning intonation patterns nor to make them conscious (or self-conscious) of their use of these patterns. Children will, however, use the patterns of intonation naturally *if they realize the meaning of what they are saying*. The *oral reading* must become the *telling* of the meaning which they have received from the written words. Their intonation will demonstrate whether they have really got that meaning or are simply pronouncing words which as a group do not for them stimulate any recognition responses.

Pictures have been excluded as a matter of principle from the readers of this series in order to force the pupils to *read* for the meanings rather than have them obtain the situational meaning from the pictures and then guess at the identity of the words that usually accompany the pictures.

The Readers of this "linguistic" series center attention upon the clues furnished by the words alone, that is, by the spelling-patterns that represent the linguistic units which the language itself uses to separate and identify the words. Pupils do not need the crutches that the ordinary use of pictures thrusts upon them. In fact, such pictures furnish a distracting element in the process of learning to read. They attract the attention of the pupil away from the spelling-patterns that must be learned and take away from him the necessity of getting the situation meanings from the sequences of the sentences to be read.

In these materials the ordinary process of starting with pictures is completely reversed. From reading the words as they appear in the sentence sequences the pupil must grasp the situation presented in the story. And then, in order to strengthen his imaginative realization of that situation, he is asked to draw pictures himself that will illustrate parts of the story. Many, even those of the slower learners, do very well with these exercises.

REFERENCES

1. Hanna, Paul, and Moore, James T. "Spelling—From Spoken Word to Written Symbol," *Elementary School Journal* LIII (Feb. 1953), 329-37. Also in *Education Digest,* May 1953, 16-19.

2. Hall, Robert A. *Sound and Spelling in English,* Chilton Company, Book Division, Philadelphia, Pa., 1961.

3. Hall, Robert A. "Graphemics and Linguistics," Symposium on Language and Culture, Proceedings of the 1962 Annual Spring Meeting of the American Ethnological Society (1963), 53-59.

4. Voegelin, C. F., and Voegelin, F. M. "Typological Classification of Systems with Included, Excluded, and Self-Sufficient Alphabets," in *Anthropological Linguistics,* III, Jan. 1961, 55-96.

5. Hanna, Paul, and Hanna, Jean Schuman. *Phoneme-Grapheme Correspondences,* (a detailed analysis of 17,000 different American English words). A Cooperative Research Project of the U. S. Office of Education, 1962.

6. Higginbottom, Eleanor. University College, London Univ., "A Study of the Representation of English Vowel Phonemes in the Orthography," *Language and Speech,* III, Pt. 2, April-June 1962.

7. Garvin, Paul, and Trager, Edith Crowell. Machine Translation of Speech into Orthographic English, Nov. 1, 1963, "The Conversion of Phonetic into Orthographic English, a Machine Translation Approach to the Problem." Final Version issued Nov. 1963, TRW Computer Division, Thompson Ramo Woolridge Inc., Canoga Park, Calif.

8. Hodges, Richard E., and Rudorf, E. Hugh. *Phoneme-Grapheme Relationships,* National Council of Teachers of English, Nov. 1964.

9. Weir, Ruth Hirsch. *Formulation of Grapheme-Phoneme Correspondence Rules to Aid in the Teaching of Reading,* (Cooperative Research Project No. S-039), Stanford University, 1964.

10. Dolby, James L., and Resnikoff, Howard L ."On the Structure of Written English Words," *Language,* 40 (1964), 167-196.

11. Various reports of studies of phoneme-grapheme correspondences from "A Basic Research Program on Reading, Cornell University, 1963." E. J. Gibson, C. F. Hockett, H. Levin, R. L. Venezky, and others.

ARTHUR W. HEILMAN

THE PENNSYLVANIA STATE UNIVERSITY

5. Phonics Emphasis Approaches

Two OBJECTIVES of this discussion are to identify salient features of a limited number of phonic approaches to beginning reading and to stress the educational issues which are related to the debate on phonics emphasis which has characterized the past decade.

Background

The problem of what is the proper role of phonics in reading instruction is not new. Undoubtedly the pressures on schools and teachers today, which are traceable to this issue are unprecedented. In general, the most vociferous critics of present day reading instruction start from a number of erroneous premises which suit their purposes. These premises include:

1. There is a sight word method of teaching reading which makes no provision for teaching phonic skills.
2. All words met at various instructional levels are taught exclusively as "sight words."
3. There is an educational conspiracy in American education which is opposed to the teaching of phonics.
4. Phonics instruction is "good" and children cannot get too much of a good thing.
5. If we go back to the phonics emphasis of the 1890's, present reading problems in our schools would disappear.

To illustrate the present state of affairs we will turn to the Council on Basic Education, a non-profit organization dedicated to the improvement of American education. In so far as the Council on Basic Education has been concerned with reading instruction, that concern has focused entirely on the issue of phonics. In the January 1964 *Bulletin* (p. 1) of the Council we read:

Perhaps the most encouraging development of the year (1963), was the

56

increasing understanding on the part of the public of what the phonics *versus* sight reading controversy is all about. The issue has often been confused in the public mind, especially when the advocates of the sight, or look-and-say method, insist that they also are believers in phonics instruction.

In the CBE *Bulletin,* February 1962 (p. 2), one finds:

> From our observation of good teachers in the fields of reading and language we discern a few guiding principles and methods of operations.
> 1. The good teacher of beginning reading, where she is not bound by an imposed methodology, operates on the theory that *beginning* reading is not a 'thought getting' process but is based on translating letters into sounds.

No evidence was cited as to source of this data.

In discussing an article by Paul Woodring, (*Saturday Review,* January 20, 1962) which made a plea for less heat and less name calling in the discussion of reading methodology, the editor of the Council's *Bulletin* stated, "It seems to us that anyone who suggests, even by indirection, that the present reading controversy does not involve fundamental issues but is merely a reflection of temperamental differences between reading theorists, misreads the true nature of the controversy. There is a real war on in reading, and for the future well-being of American education it is *important that the right side win.*" [Emphasis added.] CBE *Bulletin,* March 1962, pp. 8-9.

The individual who wants to make beginning reading a meaningful and enjoyable experience may have cause to feel threatened by the almost unlimited number of phonic systems which deal only with this limited facet of reading. This factor, coupled with the emergence of the philosophy that a "fast start" in beginning reading based on early stress of phonics is an unmitigated virtue, poses an educational issue of major importance.

The writer has long been of the opinion that phonics is second in importance to no other reading skill, and that "the reader must have the ability to pronounce or to approximate the pronunciation of words he does not know as sight words. This is ample reason for teaching phonics and sufficient justification for teaching it well" (9). Nevertheless, holding such a view does not preclude resistance to critics and materials which would push us into:

1. Teaching more phonics than is necessary for the child to learn to read.
2. Neglecting procedures for differentiation of phonics instruction.

3. Overemphasizing phonics in *beginning* reading.
4. Teaching phonics "steps" in illogical sequence.
5. Developing an over-reliance on phonics, (or context, or any other word analysis skill), as all such extremes are uneconomical and indefensible.
6. Behaving as if we believed that a child's memorizing phonic rules assures the ability to apply these rules in reading situations.

With these cautions in mind we move to a brief analysis of a limited number of phonic-emphasis approaches to first grade reading.

The Carden Method

The Carden Method is a set of materials and a methodology developed and published by Mae Carden (*4*). Although the method stresses composition and spelling, its chief aim is the teaching of phonics. Book I deals primarily with the two-vowel rule. Book II teaches the sound of single vowels, and Book III introduces combinations which include *r* and *w*. The author suggests that *after* pupils have completed the Carden readers they move on to basal readers. Thus, the initial stage of reading is saturated with letter sound analysis. This approach:

I. *Stresses Rules*

Initial teaching is limited to "regular spellings," or words which follow the given rule. The child is taught to "cross off" silent vowels and the famous two-vowel rule is modified to read: "When there are 2 vowels in a word the second vowel is crossed off and the first vowel keeps its name sound."

The following steps are utilized in teaching two-vowel patterns:

A. The term *vowel* is not used until after children have studied all vowels.
B. *a, e, i, o, u* = "The little letters that change their sounds."
C. Find the two letters that change their sounds.
　　1. Think! Which one comes first in the word and which one comes second in the word?
　　2. Cross off the one that comes second.
　　3. Sound out the word letter by letter (*coat* = cuh' o tuh).

Later a goodly number of amendments or new rules are advanced or taught. Examples:

A. "There are *ea* words where the *a* drops out." (head, bread)

B. "There are words in which the *o* drops out in the *ou* combination and has the sound of *u*." (double, trouble, country)

II. *Stresses Synthetic Sounding*

Each consonant (or digraph) is given the weight of a syllable, (b—*buh;* j—*juh;* g—*guh;* th—*thuh;* ch—*chuh;* etc.). The word *the* is pronounced *thuh* and once the sound of a few letters have been introduced the child is ready to read a sentence:

suh' e	thuh	buh' o tuh
see	*the*	*boat*

(*preprimary manual*, p. 42)

Since an ordinary three- or four-letter word is sounded as though it consists of three syllables, the teacher is instructed to place the accent on the initial letter. (*boat* = buh' o tuh; *coat* = kuh' o tuh)

III. *Stresses Writing and Spelling from the Beginning of Instruction*

The letter *c* plays an important role in the teaching of letter forms. The child is taught that:

A. "Seven letters begin with *c*." These are: *c, a, d, g, q, o, e,* (The point is that there is a *c* imbedded somewhere in each of these letters.)

B. "Two letters make a *c* backwards." These are: *b, p*.

C. "The letter *s* is a *c* up in the air and a *c* backwards."

The following is from "A Note on Learning to Spell." The teacher constructs a word letter by letter applying the two-vowel rule. Example:

The word *dime* is given.

The teacher says, "Write *duh*."

She adds, "What did you write?"

The pupils answer, *"D."*

The teacher says, "Write *i* next to the *d*."

Then she says, *"m*, write *m, m—m."*

The pupils write *m*.

The teacher asks, "How do you make the *i* stay *i*?"

The pupils answer, "Add an *e*." (*The Carden Method, A Brief on How To Get Started.*)

In the opinion of the writer, this approach is extremely mechanistic and ritualistic. However, it should not be concluded that children exposed to this type of instruction in grade one will not "learn" what is commonly measured at the end of grade one as "reading achievement." This is a tribute to children, but perhaps an unfortunate educational phenomena since the fact that "learning takes place" is often cited as a justification for the use of such procedures.

Words in Color

Words In Color (7) is a system developed by Caleb Gattegno who also developed *Numbers in Color* based on the Cuisenaire Rods for teaching arithmetic. These materials are discussed as a "phonics emphasis approach" because instruction begins and continues with the systematic teaching of letter sounds. The child is exposed to a dual visual stimuli: (1) the letter configuration, (2) in color. He hears hundreds of repetitions of each letter sound while his attention is focused on the *letter configuration* in color.

In this approach 39 colors are used, each of which represents a speech sound in English—regardless of what letters represent that sound. Initial teaching is done entirely at the blackboard using different colored chalks, and through the use of some 29 large wall charts done in color. On these charts the various letters and letter combinations in a given word are shown in different colors. Thus, the word *and* utilizes three colors; *sand,* four colors; and *impossible* calls for the use of seven colors. (The writer being color-blind could not verify this latter fact for himself, but accepted the word of a trusted colleague.)

The following are some pertinent facts about *Words In Color*:

1. Sounding, or the association of colored-letter *forms* with speech sounds, is taught in a most systematic, repetitive fashion. The term *drill* used in this setting would not be an overstatement. In the teaching of letter sounds the individual consonants are not taught in isolation but are blended with vowel sounds.

2. At this moment there is, to the best of the writer's knowledge, not a single piece of research which even hints that the addition of color to *letter forms* adds one iota to the learning of letter sounds or phonic principles.

3. The child actually never reads anything in color (except letters and words on the wall charts or in blackboard drill). All reading materials used are printed black on white!

4. Thirty-nine colors is a goodly number of colors. It is a tenable hypothesis that children might develop problems in discrimination of just noticeable differences in color in the absence of letter

configurations. Examples of one series of colors include: cadmium green, yellow green No. 15, yellow green No. 47, dark green, olive green, light green, deep green, emerald green No. 45, emerald green No. 26, leaf green, gray green, yellow ochre, brown ochre.

5. Materials include: for teachers, *Background and Principles, Teacher's Guide,* 21 Wall Charts, 8 Phonic Code Charts; and children's materials (printed black on white), Books 1, 2, 3, *First Book of Stories,* set of worksheets.

Programmed Reading *(2)*

While there are a number of materials which might merit the designation *programmed reading* our discussion is limited to one set of materials which meets the criterion of being a phonics emphasis approach to beginning reading (*Programmed Reading,* Webster Division, McGraw-Hill Book Co.). These materials are primarily a program for grades one and two, and for remedial instruction. The program begins with the teaching of word symbols which have "a constant sound value." Thus, we meet again the "word family" of previous eras or "regular spellings" of one linguistic approach.

However, before beginning to work with the programmed materials the child must have mastered a sizeable portion of word analysis or the phonic skills program which includes the following:

1. The names of the letters of the alphabet (capital and small).
2. How to print all the capital and small letters.
3. That letters stand for sounds and what sounds to associate with the letters *a, f, m, n, p, t, th,* and *i* which are used as the points of departure for the programmed readers.
4. That letters are read from left to right and that groups of letters form words.
5. The words *yes* and *no* by sight; how to discriminate the words *ant, man,* and *mat* from each other, and how to read the sentences, *I am an ant, I am a man, I am a mat, I am a pin, I am a pan, I am thin, I am tan, I am fat.*

These skills are taught in a stage called programmed pre-reading which, by the nature of what is taught, emphasizes the association of letter symbol with corresponding letter sound.

The programmed materials are workbook type exercises calling for the child to circle the correct word or write a letter or letters. For instance, a

picture of an ant is followed by the sentence: *I am an $\frac{ant}{man}$*. A later frame
will be *I am an -nt*. It should be noted that these materials rely heavily on
visual discrimination and that there is considerable emphasis on "word
parts" or individual letters.

Without doubt programmed materials hold some promise for teaching
certain facets of beginning reading. A promotional brochure heralds these
particular materials as "the most significant breakthrough in the teaching
of reading in 50 years!" This might be an overstatement. One of the
virtues of programmed learning is the fact that the child can instantly
check his response to see if he is correct. As the child writes a vowel, a
consonant blend, or a word in a blank space he can look to the left on the
same frame and see if he wrote correctly. He can also look before he writes
if he learns this approach.

One strength of programmed reading is that it could be called an
individualized approach. However, in this case every child uses the same
material or book, but each goes through it at his own rate. Programmed
materials deal with mechanical aspects of the reading process. These are
important, but they are not all there is to reading. There has been little, if
any, programming of critical reading or thought processes.

The Phonovisual Method *(14)*

The Phonovisual Method is a supplementary phonic instruction program
designed for use with existing basal and other approaches. The authors
offer their materials as a "middle course" stating, "The Phonovisual
Method is not intended to be used instead of sight reading, but as a
parallel teaching" (*14*, p. 6). As is the case with many other phonics
instructional materials there are no major differences in the "content" of
the phonics program of phonovisual and basal materials. The major
differences are:

1. The degree to which phonic teaching dominates beginning reading
   instruction.
2. The emphasis on *drill* in associating letter sounds and graphic letter
   symbols.

It should be noted that the teacher is cautioned to always use the
material as a game, not as drill. Yet, it is obvious that the amount of
emphasis on teaching letter sounds makes this a difficult goal to achieve.
"For best results the teaching [of letter sounds] should begin the very first

week of school if possible the very first day. At the demonstration school one half-hour daily is given to each of these two subjects, (a) sight reading and (b) phonetic instruction . . ." (*14*, p. 11).

Materials. The Phonovisual materials are described as a phonics program for kindergarten, primary, and remedial instruction, and include the following:

1. Two 26" x 40" wall charts—one for teaching consonant sounds, the other for vowel sounds.
2. Phonovisual method book (a teacher's guide).
3. Pupils' books: Readiness book, transition book (preprimer), separate consonant and vowel workbooks.
4. Miscellaneous items: Phonograph recording, "Sounds on the Phonovisual Charts," skill building flash cards, consonant and vowel filmstrips, magnetic boards, phonic rummy games, and the like.

Of all the numerous phonic approaches, phonovisual probably most closely parallels the philosophy of a majority of basal materials. Consonant sounds are taught first, auditory-visual training is coordinated, learning words as sight-recognition units is encouraged. One of the major potential drawbacks in the use of phonovisual is that the actual instruction can easily go beyond simply systematic teaching and become a ritual.

The matter of differentiation of amounts of phonic instruction for different pupils is not stressed. Despite the warnings of the authors, and particularly in light of the procedures outlined, the teaching of sounding can easily become an end in itself rather than the means to achieving a balanced program whose goal is fluent, critical reading. On the other hand, the materials provide a concrete step-by-step program which introduces practically all of the phonics teaching in grade one. Some teachers may profit from this systematic approach while at the same time modifying techniques so as to minimize rote teaching.

Phonetic Keys to Reading

Phonetic Keys to Reading (*8*) is a quite accurate description of the materials which bear this title. The "keys" are the multitude of "rules" that have accumulated over a number of decades as a result of attempting to deal with the vagaries of letter sounds in written English. *Phonetic Keys* provides for teaching children all of the known rules including some which have very limited application. The data reported by Clymer (*5*), Oaks (*13*), and Burrows/Lourie (*3*), relative to the per cent of time various phonic rules actually apply, should be kept in mind as prospective users attempt to evaluate the materials under discussion.

Phonetic Keys is not a method of teaching reading but a set of supplementary phonics materials. The first two months of beginning instruction are devoted to teaching approximately forty separate phonic skills including both long and short vowel sounds, all consonant sounds, and a number of blends and consonant digraphs. For the first several weeks children are taught to sound letters (vowels) which are invariably located in the middle of words. Following this unique experience they are taught initial consonant sounds.

A reasonable rationale for attacking the middle of words has never been advanced. Promotional materials point out, "Since each word contains one or more than one vowel, no words can be sounded independently by the pupil until he has a knowledge of the more common vowel sounds." It might be pointed out that all words except *I, a* and *eye* contain consonants which must be noted if the word is to be solved.

As a result of the emphasis on sounding in beginning reading the child is in essence taught, and many learn, to acquire a set to sound out words. The same word is sounded out time after time, long after it should have been mastered as a sight word. The teacher's manual in discussing the use of experience charts cautions teachers against teaching words as sight words, "At first these charts are to be read by sight, but as soon as the children have learned enough sounds and phonetic principles to analyze words with the help of the teacher, teaching experience charts and reading charts by sight should be entirely eliminated" (*Teacher's Manual for First Grade*, 1964, p. 18).

Materials. First grade materials consist of three paperback workbook-type books, *Tag, Dot and Jim, All Around with Dot and Jim,* and a teacher's manual. The materials were developed by Cornelia Sloop, an elementary teacher in Texas.

The major educational issues with which users and prospective users of these materials should be concerned include:

1. Should beginning reading instruction concentrate on sounding letters to the degree these materials advocate?
2. Should initial sounding begin in the middle of words?
3. Should children learn dozens of complicated phonic rules in the process of beginning reading?
4. Can sounding be "overemphasized" to the detriment of future reading facility?

5. Can beginning instruction result in pupils' developing a "set" to sound out each word met?

6. All facile readers recognize words as units and sound out only those few words they do not recognize as sight words. Should children be taught to sound out all words to the neglect of developing a sight vocabulary?

Linguistic Approach
(Emphasizing Speech Sounds in Words)

This discussion does not attempt to deal with all linguistic theory and suggested practices which relate to beginning reading instruction. Reference is made only to one approach, that of limiting initial teaching to words which enjoy "regular spellings" in English. While the term *phonics* might be offensive to the linguist-authors, the materials merit discussion here since their chief aim is the early association of speech sounds with written letter combinations.

The first such serious proposal by a linguist was presented publicly in 1942. The April and May issues of *The Elementary English Review* contained articles by Leonard Bloomfield in which he outlined what in essence was later published in 1961 under the title, *Let's Read—A Linguistic Approach* (*1*). Reduced to its essentials this approach simply advocates teaching beginning reading through the process of teaching words which follow "regular spellings" in English.

This approach relies on a very rigid vocabulary control. Each lesson introduces and stresses what in the past was called "word families," such as *cat, rat, fat, mat, bat, sat*. The child first learns words in isolation, then phrases and sentences: *a bat, a cat, a rat, a mat, a fat cat, a fat rat, a fat cat ran at a fat cat* (*Let's Read*, Bloomfield and Barnhart, p. 61).

In 1963, Charles Fries' book *Linguistics and Reading* was published. There are minor differences between Bloomfield's and Fries' approaches. The former advocated that children learn letter names and learn to distinguish both capital and lower case letters, while Fries advocated teaching only capital letters in beginning reading. However, in regard to methodology Fries and Bloomfield advocate almost identical content. The same words, phrases, and sentences are found in both sources, for example in Fries, *"a cat, a rat, a fat rat, pat a fat rat, cats bat at rats"* (*6,* p. 203).

Both Bloomfield and Fries (in the materials referred to above) oppose the practice of making beginning reading instruction a meaning-making process for the reader. In the words of Clarence Barnhart, coauthor of

Let's Read, we find: "Bloomfield's system of teaching reading is a linguistic system. Essentially, a linguistic system of teaching reading separates the problem of the study of word-form from the study of word-meaning" (p. 9).

In Fries we find: "Seeking an extraneous interest in a story as a story during the earliest steps of reading is more likely to hinder than to help the efforts put forth by the pupil himself" (6, p. 199)*.

When a person in reading raises questions as to the actual contributions made by linguists he is put in the position of a mere educational practitioner questioning the role of the scientist. When a linguist has reservations about the contributions of linguists to reading we might listen. Raven I. McDavid of the University of Chicago stated:

> I am diffident about how much the linguist can contribute to the complex
> operation of teaching reading, which may utilize everything from informa-
> tion theory to the doctrine of original sin. Like many of my colleagues, I am
> disturbed that linguistics is currently fashionable, often considered a panacea
> for all the woes of education and society. For with the supply of professional
> linguists low and the demand for their services high, we find a proliferation
> of store-front linguists clamoring to perform these services . . . And when
> the linguist attempts to produce readers, he can expect them to be criticized
> on both linguistic and other grounds (*10*).

The Augmented Roman Alphabet

The objective of the Augmented Roman Alphabet is to present an initial teaching medium which approximates a one-to-one relation between letter-symbol seen and speech-sound heard when a word is pronounced. To accomplish this, 19 new letter characters were added to the present English alphabet after dropping the letters *q* and *x*. (For ITA materials see Mazurkiewicz and Tanyzer, *12*.)

Some of the methodological features of this system are:

1. Phonics or letter sounds associated with graphic symbols are taught systematically and thoroughly.

---

*Certain other linguists do not reject meaning in reading. Lefevre stresses "that language is meaningful behavior and that reading is the reproduction of sound patterns which carry meanings." In addition there has been a considerable body of writing which stresses the various *signal systems.* Under this heading the linguist discusses *intonation patterns, pitch, stress, juncture, transitions, pauses,* and the like. Teachers of reading have used different terminology without neglecting these important facets. (Reading terms might be, "reading with expression," "read it like you would say it." Juncture — pause — stops would be taught as functions of punctuation and phrasing.

2. Child learns symbol sound, not letter name.
3. Children write this new symbol system from the very beginning of instruction.
4. Separate capital letters are not used. Capitals are indicated by making the letter larger.
5. Children are expected to make a transition from this initial teaching alphabet to traditional orthography and spelling within a year; four to five months for the rapid learners; seven to eight months for the average pupils. In data reported from England, the transition was reportedly made without difficulty. However, pupils transferred from Augmented Roman to the same materials printed in regular or traditional orthography.

Some Issues:

1. *Teaching children to write the Augmented Alphabet.*

A very important question is, "If the child is to transfer from the initial teaching medium to traditional in from 4 to 8 months, why should he learn and reinforce the Augmented Alphabet in his own writing?" The ITA is much more difficult to write as one meets symbols such as:

ᚢh, æ, rg, œ, ᚦh, ie, ᚄ, ɛɛ, ω.

2. *The compatibility of ITA and Traditional Orthography.*

In the promotional materials for ITA it is claimed that there is a high degree of compatibility between spellings in ITA and traditional spellings. A fact that is often overlooked is that in addition to the changed alphabet in ITA a great number of words are changed to phonetic spellings, some of which do not involve any of the new letters. The re-spellings result in visual configurations which are radically different from those the child will meet once he transfers to traditional English. This is, in essence, not a system for "cracking the code" but rather the teaching of a substitute code. Do no children experience difficulty in transferring from phonetic spellings to the traditional irrational spellings? The following examples come from one small first-grade book of less than primer difficulty.

was – woᚄ	watched – wotᚦht	walked – waukt
excited – eksieteᑯ	enough – enuf	also – aulsœ
wife – wief	sixth – siksᚦh	right – riet
called – caullᑯ	find – fienᑯ	thought – ᚦhaut
large – larj	crossed – crosst	next – nekst
pleased – plɛɛᐤᑯ	climb – cliem	boxes – bokseᚄ
busy – biᚄy	night – niet	George – jorj
quieter – kwieter	castles – caslᚄ	six – siks

(a seesied holidæ for jæn and tœby, ann fhwaite, cunstabl and cumpany limited, lundon.)

In the promotional material the question is asked, "Is the traditional alphabet and spelling of English an important cause of failure in beginning reading?" It might be stated that failures do not stem primarily from the traditional alphabet, but from spellings of words. As noted above, ITA does not rely solely on a new alphabet but actually utilizes a considerable number of re-spellings of English words.

ITA actually attempts to follow the traditional "rules" found in most phonic approaches, particularly with regard to the "two vowel" and "one vowel in medial position" rules. When words do not follow the rules they are spelled phonetically:

one—wun	half—hav	come—cum
some—sum	have—hav	money—muny
said—sed	head—hed	once—wunz
more—mor	were—wer	

3. Emphasis on teaching Phonics

A point that is seldom stressed on the popular writings about ITA is the fact that in this approach sounding or phonic analysis is taught both early and systematically. A large number of letters (consonants) are the same in structure and sound in both the augmented and traditional alphabets (b, d, f, h, j, k, m, n, p, r, t, y). The digraphs *ch, th, sh, wh* have the same sound and are very similar in visual pattern, although joining the two symbols in writing is more difficult.

The early stress on sounding or phonic analysis thus becomes a contaminating factor in research which purports to demonstrate that use of the Augmented Alphabet is the primary independent variable in comparative studies. The efficacy of the Augmented Alphabet could be tested only if the traditional alphabet approach with which it is compared included the same amount of early phonics emphasis.

4. Results of instruction using ITA

There have been many reports in the popular press which contain suggestions, intimations and projections which often result in a reader's inferring that initial instruction using ITA, followed by transfer to traditional print sometime in grade one, will lead to significantly higher reading achievement at the end of grade one. The data covering the Bethlehem, Pennsylvania study, 1963-64, reported by Mazurkiewicz does not bear out this assumption, although that writer's tentative conclusions continue to be optimistic.

There was no significant difference in reading achievement between groups taught by ITA and traditional basal instruction:

TABLE I (*11*)

Total Raw Scores	ITA Mean	S.D.	Traditional Mean	S.D.	T. Test
California Reading Test (Lower Primary)	59.60	17.42	61.15	16.15	0.433
California Reading Test (Upper Primary)	41.11	19.28	41.29	16.90	0.064

Summary: The above phonic emphasis approaches cannot justifiably be labeled "methods of teaching reading." Each deals primarily with one important reading skill, namely, phonic analysis. To qualify as a method a set of materials would have to embrace a broad teaching program which attempts to deal with all of the essential skills which need to be taught in the entire program. A second criterion of a method would be that learning to read would of necessity be treated as a developmental process, extending over a relatively long period of time.

Each of the above approaches, as is the case with other phonic materials not discussed, deals only with beginning reading and attempts to saturate this instructional period with analysis of letter sounds. This extensive and intensive drill on sounding letters often has a salutary effect on reading achievement scores during the early stages of formal instruction. Standardized reading tests for grade one deal primarily with word recognition, and thus tend to measure what phonics-emphasis approaches teach.

Reading vocabularies of pupils at this stage of development do not approximate their capacity for dealing with oral language. The point of view of this paper is that this fact of human development does not serve as a justification for the position that beginning reading need not be a meaning-making process. Language is a system of agreements as to the meaning ascribed to particular speech sounds *as found in words and words-in-combination.* Meaning is the only thing that *can* transfer from oral language usage to facile reading of the graphic representation of oral language.

This question, as to whether beginning reading should be a meaning-making process is one of the major educational issues in the present controversy over the proper role of phonics instruction. Starting from the premise that *students must acquire the ability to sound out words not recognized as sight words,* other questions teachers of reading should answer as they think of methology and materials are:

1. When initial reading instruction centers on letter-sound analysis is it not likely that a number of pupils will develop a "set" to sound out all words met?
2. Will some pupils continue to sound out the same words long after they should have been mastered as sight words?
3. Is it not true that smooth, facile reading is characterized by a minimum of recourse to "sounding out words"?
4. Do some phonic-instructional materials overemphasize what teaching letter sounds can actually accomplish in reading English?
5. Does the large number of irregular spellings in English mitigate against teaching over-reliance on sounding?
6. Do phonic instruction materials tend to under-emphasize the value of combining phonic analysis and context clues in solving unknown words?
7. If a set of materials and instructional procedures results in higher first-grade reading achievement, is this *prima facie* evidence that this approach is a better learning experience than any approach which achieves lesser results over this relatively short segment of the total educational continuum?
8. Specifically, is the "fast start" which may accrue from hours of drill on analyzing letter sounds inevitably the best *introduction* to the long-term developmental process called *learning to read?*

The point of view emphasized in this presentation is that the educational issues in phonics instruction center around (1) initial learning *set* which materials develop; (2) that letter-sound analysis is limited by the nature of written English; (3) over-reliance on phonics can be taught; (4) that not to use all word-analysis clues (context, structure, pictures) is uneconomical; (5) the sequence in which steps are taught should be based on a psychologically sound rationale.

If one concludes that numerous phonic approaches err in saturating initial reading instruction with letter-sound analysis, and over-emphasize what this can accomplish in learning to read English, the original premise still remains intact. Namely, that children must learn sounding techniques and that these should be taught effectively.

Simply because approaches A, B, C, etc. over-emphasize analysis in beginning reading does not establish that materials which present much less phonic analysis have hit upon the "right combination." To not systematically teach vowel sounds in grade one is a methodological decision which handicaps a majority of pupils in first grade.

All reading-instructional-materials are offsprings of the free enterprise system. Promotional materials which describe and sell reading materials are often much more imaginative than the materials themselves. "Let the buyer beware" applies as well to the adoption of teaching materials as it does to the purchase of a used car. Education will have nothing to fear from this philosophy and practice when teachers and administrators develop the professional competency to ask the right questions and evaluate materials in light of their questions.

REFERENCES

1. Bloomfield, Leonard, and Barnhart, Clarence L. *Let's Read—A Linguistic Approach,* Detroit: Wayne State University Press, 1961.
2. Buchanan, Cynthia Dee, *et. al. Programmed Reading.* St. Louis: Webster Division, McGraw-Hill Book Co., 1963.
3. Burrows, Alvina T., and Lourie, Zyra. "Two Vowels Go Walking," *The Reading Teacher,* XVII, (November 1963).
4. Carden, Mae. *The Carden Method.* Glen Rock, New Jersey.
5. Clymer, Theodore. "The Utility of Phonic Generalizations in the Primary Grades," *The Reading Teacher,* XVI, (January 1963).
6. Fries, Charles C. *Linguistics and Reading.* New York: Holt, Rinehart and Winston, Inc., 1963.
7. Gattegno, Caleb. *Words in Color.* Chicago: Learning Materials, Inc., 1962.
8. Harris, Theodore, Creekmore, Mildred, and Greenman, Margaret. *Phonetic Keys to Reading.* Oklahoma City: The Economy Company, 1964.
9. Heilman, Arthur W. *Phonics in Proper Perspective.* Columbus, Ohio: Charles E. Merrill Books, Inc., 1964.
10. McDavid, Raven I., Jr. "Linguistics and Reading," *Reading and the Language Arts,* Supplementary Educational Monograph No. 93, University of Chicago Press, 1963.
11. Mazurkiewicz, Albert J. "Lehigh-Bethlehem ITA Study Interim Report Six," *Journal of the Reading Specialist,* Vol. 4 (September 1964).
12. Mazurkiewicz, Albert J., and Tanyzer, Harold. *ITA Program.* New York: ITA Publications, Inc., 1963.
13. Oakes, Ruth E. "A Study of the Vowel Situations in a Primary Vocabulary," *Education,* LXXII (May 1952).
14. Schoolfield, Lucille D., and Timberlake, Josephine B. *Phonovisual Method.* Washington, D.C.: Phonovisual Products, Inc.

EDWARD FRY

RUTGERS — THE STATE UNIVERSITY

6. New Alphabet Approaches

PERHAPS the most provable thing about new alphabet approaches is that they are not new at all. One need only scratch the surface of a library, and a cornucopia of revised alphabets, spelling reforms, and diacritical marking plans for beginning reading pours forth.

The history of the development of written language is exceedingly voluminous. There is no time in recorded history when it was not under attack and change. Probably the invention of movable type and the printing press has done more to slow down the change in written language in the last few centuries than any other single factor. In these last few centuries we have attained a high degree of rigidity in written language. We now find ourselves in the somewhat strange position of having dictionaries largely agree on exactly what letters should be used to spell each word in our language; it has not always been thus.

We could start a discussion of the need and desirability of new alphabets with a look at Cuniform and Linear B, but let us jump ahead thirty centuries to the annual report of the National Education Association in 1910.

> Your committee is able to make a report of progress that is very encouraging to those interested in the simplification of the spelling of English, as the year has been notable in the things that have been done and in the cooperation that has been secured. . . . The ridicule and the contumely heaped upon the movement five years ago has almost entirely disappeared, and the opposition to a reasonable consideration of its demands and claims is gone.

Alas the bright hopes of the educators of 1910 have been dashed on the hard rocks of history. The whole problem of alphabet reform or spelling reform is largely a political one. Any scholar could singlehandedly improve English spelling or the alphabet. However, the problem is that people with power—presidents, senators, giant corporations who publish books, even

72

adults who vote—do not want a change because they already know the established system. On the other hand, the people who really need the change, the first-graders and the adult illiterates, have virtually no power at all. Apparently the education profession has very little power in this grave matter either.

The Reader's Problem

Lest one feel that we have gotten off the track by discussing simplified spelling in a new alphabet approaches article, let us put the whole area in "perspective." The basic problem of the first grade teacher is to train the child to decode a set of symbols which constitutes what we call written language. This set of symbols is rather closely based on spoken language. The average first grade child already possesses a good knowledge of spoken language. His vocabulary is something in excess of 5,000 words and his knowledge of the rules and structure of the English language is amazingly good. An interesting proof of the first-grader's facility with structure is to compare him with a newly arrived foreign university student who, even though well-educated, uses torturous and often erroneous sentence structures and intonations.

Since it is the problem of the first grade student to learn to decode the written symbols, quite obviously the manner in which the language is incoded will have a profound effect. If the symbols follow strange and highly irregular principles it stands to reason that the child will have greater difficulty learning to decode them. Hence, anything that will improve the coding system, even temporarily, for beginning readers has been a concern of educators and many other intelligent people for at least centuries and probably for as long as there has been inaccurate coding systems. Thus, new alphabets, spelling reforms, and devices which temporarily add regularity, such as diacritical marks, are all part of our problem. Spelling is simply the obverse of the same problem—that of incoding, or having to write the symbol, as opposed to decoding, or having to read the symbol.

The Alphabet Problem

A good bit of the problem of incoding English developed during the 15th century in what scholars call "the great vowel shift." In this period between Chaucer and Shakespeare spoken English went through a noticeable change while written English failed to keep abreast. It was towards the end of this period that the spelling of English became somewhat crystallized due to dictionary makers like Samuel Johnson and technical innovators like Gutenberg.

The situation was further compounded by the inadequacy of the sound symbols or alphabet that the English chose to use. The alphabet which we use is really designed for writing Latin, not English. Hence, we note that modern Latin or Spanish and Italian have far fewer problems in spelling than does English. There are something like 44 different phonemes or distinctive sound units used in speaking English; however, our alphabet has only 26 letters and at least three of these are no good at all as they overlap or duplicate the work of other letters (*C* sounds like an *S* or a *K*, *X* sounds like *KS*, and *Q* is used only with *U* and sounds like *KW*).

We get around this problem of an inadequate number of letters several ways. In consonants the situation is not too bad as we tend to use digraphs, or a special combination of two letters, to make a different phoneme. For example *CH* does not make a blend of *C* and *H*, but almost always makes the sound heard at the beginning of *chair*. But in the vowel sounds the situation is much more unpleasant, in that one letter makes many sounds. For example note the *A* in *at, all, above, ate*.

A Backward Glance

It will perhaps help to put the modern systems in better perspective if we have a quick trip through some historical antecedents.

In 1551 John Hart wrote an essay entitled "The Opening of the Unreasonable Writing of our English Toung." He later followed this up by suggesting a new orthography, and by 1517 he had zeroed in on the first grade problem with "A Methode of Comfortable Beginning for All Unlearned, Whereby They May Bee Taught To Read English, In A Very Short Time, With Pleasure." In the next century Charles Butler (1634) developed a phonetic alphabet for overcoming "uncertain writing and difficulty in learning." Because he found that the Latin Alphabet was "troublesome to the novice reader and writer."

America's own Benjamin Franklin, that intelligent dabbler in many things, developed in 1786 his own reformed alphabet. While technically not very good, he did see the need for consistency and the addition of six new letters. Franklin's alphabet apparently never received any acceptance but he did manage to carry on a small correspondence using it.

Leaping ahead another century, we find that Benn Pitman was producing phonetic readers for the American school market using a greatly

modified alphabet. Another 19th century innovation was Fonotypy, a
phonetically regular alphabet developed by Isaac Pitman and A. J. Ellis
in 1884.

We have already noted the interest in spelling reforms around the turn

HISTORICAL "NEW" ALPHABETS
AND
DIACRITICALLY MARKED READERS

ĭt   stănd   Ann's

ĭş   lămp   măt

              ĭ

a mat   the stand

See the lamp! It is on a mat.
The mat is on the stand.

MC GUFFEY 1881

The Eafieſt and Speedieſt-way, both for the
true fpelling and reading of Engliſh, as
alfo for the Trüe-writing thereof :
that ever was publickly
known to this day.

HODGES 1644

Hwen Jərj Woʃ-iŋ-ton woz
a-bʏt siks yerz old, hiz ʃq-der
gav him a haç-et, ov hwiç he woz
ver-i fond, and woz kon-stant-li

BENN PITMAN 1855

*Diir Madam :—ħi abdʃekʃyn.iu meek to rektifyiiŋ
aur alfabet, "ħat it uil bi atended uiħ inkanviniensiz
and difikyltiz," iz e natural uyn ; far it aluaz akyrz
huen eni refarmeʃyn is propozed ; hueħyr in rilidʃyn,*

BENJAMIN FRANKLIN 1768

Wuns upon a tʌm litɔl rɛd
hɛn livd in a barn wiΔ hʊr
fʌv ɛiks. A pig, a kʌt ʌnd

ISAAC PITMAN & A.V. ELLIS   FONOTYPY 1844

But the atţic window̸ was pănₑless.   In eămₑ the
weşt wind.   Down to the fīrₑ wĕnt the litₜlₑ girls.
They did not want any sickness.

EDWARD WARD 1894

of the century. From that time until this very day there are a number of
simplified spelling organizations which actively correspond with each other
in simplified spelling and regularly induce some local congressman to put
a bill before the United States Congress ordering that spelling in all
government documents be simplified, or proposing to write into law some
other scheme which will insure the modification of the American English
written language.

CURRENTLY USED NEW ALPHABET AND DIACRITICALLY MARKED FIRST GRADE MATERIALS

Sample of Primer
Printed in ITA

"dœn't run awæ," ben sed tω his cat.

"dœn't fiet," miek sed tω his cat.

"wæt heєr," sed ben and miek.

"weє will beє at scωl."

Sample of Primer
Printed with DMS

"Lòøk, Bill," så̇id Lindå.

"Hērȼ cỏmȩs Riȼky.

Hē is̱ åll reȧdy fôr scħöøl.

Lòøk up and sēȼ funny Riȼky."

Sample of Primer
Printed in Unifon

⊥EN M⧾CT3R H⧾Pꓷ TRⱯD. HI

P⧾KT UP BⱯBI HꞕB3RT. HELD

H⧾M ⧾N H⧾Z B⧾G ORMZ AND CAИ

U LULUBⱯ.

Sample from first drill
book for use with
Words in Color

t

at   ta   ut   tu

it   ti   et   te

ot   to

England too has had its full share of alphabet and spelling reformers. No less a celebrity than George Bernard Shaw was so seriously interested in spelling reform that he left a major proportion of his estate to a trust which now is working on the simplification of the alphabet.

In the late 1950's Sir James Pitman, the head of the publishing firm and a member of Parliament, introduced a bill for greatly modifying the English alphabet. This bill was defeated before it became law but, more or less as a direct consequence, Sir James did receive the blessing of the Minister of Education to experiment with An Augmented Roman Alphabet in the British Schools.

Some British parents, being not too well versed in the history of their language, prefer not to have their children learning from a "Roman Alphabet." Hence, the name of this new alphabet was changed to Initial Teaching Alphabet, or as it is popularly called the ITA. The name also reflects the current usage of this alphabet, namely that it is to be used for beginning instruction in literacy and later a transition is made to the traditional alphabet which ITA people like to call TO for Traditional Orthography. Though it would be impolitic to say so publicly, there is probably at least a secret thought in the minds of some supporters that ITA could become *the* English alphabet to be used by everybody at all times. Needless to say, one clever way of gaining acceptance for this would be to raise a generation of children who had equal facility in TO and ITA. Some future decades from now there might be considerably less resistance to changing spelling or an alphabet if the Prime Minister, the cabinet members, the senators, the heads of corporations and a sizeable portion of the population all had equal reading and writing facility in ITA.

An interesting thing about ITA is the wide acceptance of it before adequate research results are reported. Most of the research results (see bibliography) are reported by investigators who are closely identified with the ITA movement and in many instances have authored or published materials in the ITA medium. These research results are almost uniformly glowing. Typical reports show that teachers using the ITA materials have results that are definitely superior to other teachers using the old basal reader or traditional system. While we cannot deny that high reading achievement is a good thing no matter how it is obtained, it is something else again to prove that the superior results were due to this particular alphabet rather than the fact that a new method was used.

United States educators have recently had a multitude of claims from super-phonics enthusiasts. There is little doubt that some teacher who has been graying along through her basal reading series and suddenly gets inspired by the new super-duper phonics system is going to get better results. In fact, she would probably get as good results if the situation were reversed and all the humdrum ordinary teachers were using phonics systems and she suddenly discovered a super-duper new hot-shot word reading method. In fact, it must be a little discouraging for the educational researcher to learn that in 1851 the Massachusetts Teachers Association appointed a committee to consider the subject of "Phonetics" and that this committee reported in 1852 that teachers should study the merits of the phonetic system by themselves by actual trial in their schools. When one sees such a basic problem in existence for well over a century and yet so completely unresolved, the problem of whether or not a new alphabet will really prove superior can hardly be expected to be solved in the next few years.

The Initial Teaching Alphabet is a 43 character alphabet. It uses 24 Roman or Latin characters that are used in traditional English (X and Q are missing) plus 19 augmented or additional letters. Most of the new letters are formed by a fusion of two lower case Roman letters. Five of these new letters, the long vowels, are made by placing a lower case E immediately adjacent to the preceding vowel. Dipthongs, other vowel sounds, and consonant digraphs are frequently similarly formed by placing two letters in close juxtaposition. Writing in the ITA is also constrained by a special set of spelling rules. Hence, some words using no new letters look different because of the spelling rules only. Both the new letters and the spelling rules add a further constraint in that so far as possible traditional word form is preserved so that in a later stage of training the students may transfer to the traditional orthography with a minimum of difficulty.

In an early paper Pitman estimated that 39.25 per cent of the words were radically changed when written in ITA, 10.50 per cent were moderately changed, 23.75 per cent had minor modifications, and 26.50 per cent were unchanged. The goal of ITA is to have a consistent phoneme-grapheme relationship so that one letter will always make the same sound, and vice versa. This goal is not always achieved, partially because of the concessions to word form, but it is a tremendous improvement over the traditional orthography.

Despite the lack of conclusive research results, the spread of the use of the Initial Teaching Alphabet has been extremely rapid. The first regular use of the ITA in the public school was in Britain in September of 1960.

The experimental population consisted of approximately 600 four- and five-year-olds. The British begin reading instruction a year earlier than the Americans. In the school year 1964-65 Pitman Publishing Company, the main publishers of Initial Teaching Alphabet materials, estimates that there were approximately 60,000 British children using ITA. ITA use in the United States began in 1962 in the Bethlehem, Pennsylvania school system with a Ford Foundation grant to Dr. Albert Mazurkiewicz at Lehigh University. During the school year 1964-65 the author estimates that approximately 10,000 United States children were learning to read using the ITA. Most of these children were taking part in either continuing research in the Bethlehem schools or in research projects sponsored by the U. S. Office of Education. However, there are also many school systems "trying it out" without special foundation or government research grants. Despite these seemingly large numbers this is still far less than one per cent of the U. S. first grade population.

Words in Color

Another British import aimed at taking advantage of some phonetic regularity principles is the Words In Color system by Caleb Gattegno. This system which has been commercially available for the past five years is used by fewer schools than is the ITA. Proponents of the Gattegno system also make some interesting statements such as, "Words In Color makes the English language phonetic through the use of color, enabling the learner to master the mechanics of reading in eight weeks or less." Forty-seven different sounds of English are taught by using different colors for each sound. Since it is difficult for children, or even adults, to distinguish 47 different colors some of Gattegno's symbols are split in half so that they are really two-colored rather than a unique color. This system does not have the color printed in children's workbook material, but rather there are 21 drill charts containing 270 letters or letter groups that make a phoneme and some phonetically regular words. The teacher drills the student to make the sounds in isolation, then blended together. For example, the first page of the first book simply contains a number of A's of various sizes. The second page consists of a number of U's. The third page consists of groups of A's and U's together which the student would blend as a word. After the five vowels are introduced (short sounds), consonants are introduced and the student can now begin to blend vowels and consonants to form short meaningful and meaningless words. The teacher is also instructed to get a large selection of colored chalk so that she can write letters and words on the board for drill.

Spache points out that this idea for the use of color to identify the common sounds was introduced by Nellie Dale in 1899.

The memorization of the 47 different sounds with their corresponding colors, as well as the 270 letter combinations which commonly are used in writing these sounds, appears at least on the surface to be the heighth of a mechanical memorization approach to beginning reading. Demonstrations put on by the publisher, Encyclopaedia Britannica, managed to be interesting and lively but, as yet, research proof is lacking for the superiority of this method over any other.

Diacritical Marks

Diacritical marking plans to aid beginning readers are not exactly new. One of the oldest currently-used languages, Hebrew, has a system of marks used to indicate vowel sounds for beginning readers. After a certain degree of reading maturity is established, the marks vanish and the reader and writer use only consonants.

In 1644 an English schoolmaster Richard Hodges developed a set of diacritical marks to be used with beginning readers which the publisher put forth as, "The easiest and speediest way both for the true spelling and reading of English as also the true writing thereof that was ever publicly known to this day."

In the 1890's E. G. Ward authored a set of diacritically marked beginning reading texts published by the Silver Burdett Company for the American schools. In addition to diacritical marks that made the letters-sound relationship much more regular, Ward also underlined groups of letters that were "Phonograms."

A large number of readers in the 19th century, including the famous McGuffey series, used diacritical marks for the introduction of new words.

In 1964 Edward Fry published an article in *Elementary English* describing the Diacritical Marking System (DMS) to be used for beginning reading instruction. Later that year an experiment was begun, using the DMS marks on the Allyn & Bacon readers, in seven first grades. This Diacritical Marking System has over 99 per cent phoneme-grapheme regularity and aims to achieve essentially the same goals as the Initial Teaching Alphabet without distortion in word form or change in spelling.

The DMS is somewhat simpler than diacritical marking systems found in most dictionaries, since the intention is to aid beginning readers rather than give extreme accuracy. Regular consonants and short vowels are not marked since these are the most common usages of the letters. Long vowels have a bar over them. Regular two-letter combinations which make unique sounds such as the consonant digraphs and dipthongs, have a bar under both letters. Silent letters have a slash mark through them. These marks plus a few others, such as those used for the broad *A* and other sounds of *U,* constitute the bulk of the marks used. Nearly every word the child sees in the first grade reading books is marked and likewise all work that the teacher duplicates or puts on the board has the DMS marks. In writing children have the option of using the marks or not.

Uniphon

Another new phonetically-regular alphabet currently being used with some experiments in the Chicago area is Uniphon, developed by John Malone. This 40 letter alphabet, which the author calls "a single sound alphabet," uses block letters which have an additional interesting characteristic of being specially designed so that they can be read by computers for automatic translating purposes.

Simplified Use of Latin Alphabet

Though not really new alphabets, there are several systems of beginning reading instruction which achieve a high degree of initial phoneme-grapheme regularity by simply carefully selecting the words used in initial instruction. For example, under one type of "linguistic approach" that is put forth by Bloomfield and Barnhart, the child uses only regular consonants and short vowels. The introduction of new words is further graded so that only one short vowel is introduced per lesson. This method of controlled introduction of regular letters, while purported to be "new" in some circles, actually has as very close historical antecedent in the McGuffey Readers of the 1850's which used a similar introduction of sounds and words in its primers. While a number of other readers of the 1800's used a similar approach, one unique variation was used in the books written with words of *one syllable* published by McLoughlin Brothers in 1901. Whole books were written using only one syllable words.

Methodology

New alphabet approaches to beginning reading have some strong inferences for methodology but in and of themselves are only partially a method. For example, the most widely used set of ITA readers in the United States, written by Albert Mazurkiewicz and Harold Tanzer, have a relatively strong emphasis on the "language arts approach." These materials, which consist chiefly of a set of paperbound books with interesting stories not greatly different from a basal series, tend to have a relatively stronger *phonic* emphasis, but much of the uniqueness of method is due to the emphasis on children's writing activities in the teachers manual. While the authors would claim that it is the regularity of the ITA alphabet which facilitates children's ability to write, nonetheless the emphasis on the language arts approach is not unique to the type of alphabet used.

The DMS methods used in the current experimentation are largely overlays on the basal series. The actual pages from a basal series have been reproduced after marks have been added. The same basal series teachers manual is available, in fact required, for the teacher's use. The chief methodological feature of the DMS instructional program is the use of a number of phonic charts which accompany the basal series manual. Each time a new story is introduced in a preprimer or primer a small chart is introduced which explains one letter and its corresponding sound. The chart contains a key word (for example the word *cat* with a picture of a cat) plus several other common words which use the letter being discussed. Regular consonants and short vowels are thus introduced at the rate of one per reading lesson, and gradually digraphs, second sounds of consonants, and other vowel sounds are introduced with DMS marks. After a chart has been introduced, it is left hanging in the rooms so that the children may refer to the chart when coming across a new word. For example, if a child comes across a new word beginning with the letter *L* and he cannot remember the sound made by the letter, he needs only to look up on the board and find the *L* chart with its key picture; he may do the same with each of the letters in the word.

Conclusion

At the present time active experimentation is going on in the United States using the Initial Teaching Alphabet (ITA), the Diacritical Marking System (DMS), Uniphon, Words In Color, and the gradual introduction of phonetically regular letters—sometimes referred to as the linguistic approach. Of the new alphabets the only one which has published research reports is the Initial Teaching Alphabet. These published research reports, both from the United States and England, show that the ITA is definitely superior to the "old method." Whether or not this superiority is due to the special characteristics of ITA or the fact that it is a "new method" has yet to be established.

Three of these methods, ITA, DMS, and the linguistic approach, are being included in the large U. S. Office of Education Coordinated First Grade Reading Research Projects, a study now under way. The other two methods, Uniphon and Words In Color are being given field experimentation by their authors or publishers. Hence, all of these methods are being given classroom experimentation using method A classroom *vs.* method B classroom type of research design. While this type of research design may yield some interesting information, it is also quite possible for it to yield conflicting information such as we have seen coming from the phonics studies over the last hundred years. It is possible that for additional valuable information the reading researcher is going to have to team up with the experimental psychologist or learning researcher who designs much smaller and much more carefully controlled studies. For example, is ITA superior to the basal reader method because it is new and because it uses a language experience approach or because it uses a phonetically regular alphabet? Current investigations will probably not satisfactorily answer this question.

A further important question might be, "If ITA or DMS or any of the other systems is superior to the traditional method, is the ITA or the DMS the best method of achieving these goals?" While each of the methods that we have discussed has gone through some developmental gesticulation, each of them is essentially the work of one man. Hence, if one of the new alphabets turns out to be definitely superior to the traditional alphabet the next question should be, "Is this the best possible alphabet to do this type of job?" American educators should seek the answer to this question before any large scale adoption of a beginning reading method utilizing a new alphabet is seriously contemplated. It is perhaps a necessary step in the evolution of new ideas that there be reasonably widespread interest in the current new alphabets and classroom experimentations of the type now under way. However, for the education profession to demonstrate itself to have achieved a reasonable degree of maturity, much more money should now be spent for research and development of new alphabets rather than wide scale adoption of them.

REFERENCES

1. Downing, J. A. *The ITA Reading Experiment.* London: Evan Brothers, Ltd., 1964.
2. Downing, J. A. *Experiments With An Augmented Alphabet for Beginning Readers in British Schools.* Pamphlet published on a talk to the 27th Educational Conference sponsored by the Educational Records Bureau, New York, November 1962.
3. Downing, J. A. "The Value of ITA," *NEA Journal.* Ivan Rose, Part 1; Warren Cutts, Part 2.
4. Downing, J. A. *The Augmented Roman Alphabet. A New Two-Stage Method to Help Children to Learn to Read.* Thirteen page pamphlet printed at Pitman Press, Bath, England, undated, circa 1962.
5. Downing, J. A. *Too Bee Or Not To Be, The Augmented Roman Alphabet.* London: Cassell and Company, Ltd., 1962.
6. Downing, J. A. The I.T.A. (Initial Teaching Alphabet) Reading Experiment. *The Reading Teacher,* November 1964.
7. Franklin, Benjamin. "A Scheme For A New Alphabet And Reformed Mode Of Spelling With Remarks And Examples Concerning The Same and An Inquiry Into Its Uses In A Correspondence Between Miss Stephenson and Dr. Franklin Written In The Characters Of The Alphabet," 1768, reprinted in *Complete Works of Benjamin Franklin,* John Bigelow, Editor, G. P. Putnam's Sons, New York, 1887.
8. Fries, Charles C. *Linguistics and Reading.* New York: Holt, Rinehart & Winston, Inc., 1962.
9. Fry, Edward. "A Diacritical Marking System To Aid Beginning Reading Instruction," *Elementary English,* May 1964.
10. Gattegno, Caleb. "Words in Color" (mimeographed). Chicago: Learning Materials Inc., circa 1963.
11. Harrison, Maurice. *The Story of the Initial Teaching Alphabet.* London: Pitman Publishing Co., 1965.
12. Hodges, Richard. *The English Primrose.* London: Richard Cotes, 1644.
13. Keller, Linda. *Herbert The Hippo* (children's book in Uniphon). Chicago: Peppermint Press, Inc., 1962.
14. Mazurkiewicz, Albert J. "The Lehigh-Bethlehem ITA Study" (First Year), ITA Report, mimeographed, undated, circa 1964.
15. Mazurkiewicz, Albert J. "Teaching Reading in America Using the Initial Teaching Alphabet," *Elementary English,* November 1964.
16. National Education Association. *Journal of Procedures & Addresses.* Winona, Minnesota: 1910.
17. Pitman, Benn. *First Phonetic Reader.* Cincinnati: American Phonetic Publishing Association, 1855.

18. Pitman, Sir James. *The Ehrhardt Augmented (40 sound-42 character) lower-case Roman Alphabet.* The reasons and intentions underlying its design together with a specimen. Twenty-three page printed pamphlet. London: Pitman House, 1959.

19. Pitman, Sir James. "Learning to Read," *Journal of the Royal Society of Arts,* February 1961.

20. Pitman, Sir James. "Learning to Read. A Suggested Experiment," *The Times Educational Supplement,* May 29, 1959.

21. Pitman, Sir James. "Spelling With The Augmented Roman Alphabet." Ten-page mimeographed pamphlet circulated by Mr. Downing at teacher training meetings.

22. Pitman, Sir James. "The Future of the Teaching of Reading," *Keeping Abreast of the Revolution in Education,* edited by Arthur E. Traxler. Report of the 28th Educational Conference, American Council on Education, 1964.

23. Spache, George D. "Interesting Books for the Reading Teacher," *The Reading Teacher,* April 1964.

24. Ward, Edward R. *The Rational Method of Reading,* First Reader. Silver, Burdett & Co., Boston, 1894.

25. No author. *McGuffey's Eclectic Primer,* Revised Edition, copyright 1909, Henry H. Vail, American Book Company, New York.

RUSSELL G. STAUFFER

UNIVERSITY OF DELAWARE

7. A Language Experience Approach

O NE OF THE CONCEPTS most teachers of reading agree on is the belief that there is no one single method of teaching reading to all pupils. Those teachers who believe in the Language Arts-Experience Approach heartily endorse this educational axiom. They do so, not in spite of their belief in the Language Arts-Experience Approach, but rather because of it. This approach is not a single method but represents an integration of conditions all of which are rightly a part. *Language arts* encompasses the four facets of language and is founded on the social-personal foundation of purposeful communication. *Experience* encompasses an individual's perceptual and conceptual world; his interests, curiosities, creativity; his culture; and his capacity to adjust, to learn, and to use.

Other conditions even though quite commonplace warrant repeating and reestablishing. *First* and undoubtedly foremost is the fact that among typical six-year-olds the range of individual differences is at least five years. This means that if reading instruction is to be paced even in part on an ability grouping basis or otherwise, the range and frequency of pupil distribution has to be determined and dealt with. *Second,* reading is not only to be thought of as a communication process but also to be taught that way. Meaning is the important thing—not saying words. Reading is a thinking process and not a parroting process. *Third,* individualized reading procedures as well as group reading procedures are to be used. *Fourth,* written materials used must convey meaning in much the same way as does the oral communication of six-year-olds. Stilted artificiality must be avoided and no excuse trumped up for its use. *Fifth,* the vocabulary, the concepts, and cognitive processes that children have developed for oral communication purposes must be utilized to the fullest degree possible by linking written words as the stimulus to trigger the same concepts. *Sixth,* word attack skills need to be taught as a "first-aid" to meaning. Words

86

must be introduced in a communication context so that, as the reader moves along, meaning clues to recognition may also be a first order, functional source of help. Phonic elements must be taught in a pronunciation unit or context and not in isolation. *Seventh,* pupil interests, experiences, and knowledge must be used as a basic source of funds and must be extended and refined. *Eighth,* reading skills must be taught and paced in such a way that individuals are able to assimilate them and use them. *Ninth,* the rules of the psychology of learning must be observed. *Tenth,* the freedom and responsibilities of self-selection must be initiated from the beginning. *Eleventh,* a love of and appreciation for what reading can do for people must be fostered.

Getting Started

Most children come to first grade eager to read. The few that can read will want to show that they can do so. Others will be eager to show that they want to try. An immediate or early start should be made. The object of the start is to show pupils that reading is no more than talk written down.

A good way to accomplish all of this is by means of a pupil-dictated experience story. Arrange to have available in the room some item that will catch and hold the interest of the pupils. One teacher got under way by using a white mouse. Obviously this was unusual, but this contributed to its value as an attention-getting device and a means of stimulating oral language. There are many other similar ideas that could be used: a puppy, a chick, a baby rabbit, a parrot, a novel toy, a well-illustrated book for children such as *Hop on Pop,* or a story well told.

In the instance referred to the teacher placed the cage of the white mouse in the center of a pupil-viewing-level high table. The pupils gathered around and watched the mouse move about in his cage. They saw him stand up on his back legs with his front paws up on the side of the cage. They saw him eat from his food tin. Then the teacher took the mouse out of the cage and allowed him to walk along the top of the desk. She showed no concern about handling the mouse and her confidence and poise very much influenced the class.

As the pupils watched they talked and exclaimed: "Look, he's standing up!" "He has pink eyes." "See, how long his tail is!" When this comment was made, the teacher asked the class to say how long they thought the tail was. Estimates were given that ranged from six inches to four feet. Regardless, the teacher-question had caused all to look again and to look with a purpose.

"What should we name him?" asked the teacher. This evoked a number of interesting responses such as: "Whitey," "Snow White," "Pink Eyes." Of the different names given the class preferred "Snow White."

Now the teacher put the mouse back into the cage, covered the cage, and set it aside. Then she gathered the class around an easel on which she had tacked a large piece of newsprint. (Newsprint is pieces of lined paper approximately 2 feet by 3 feet in size.) After writing the name preferred by the class, *Snow White*, on the top line, she invited them to tell about the mouse, indicating that she would write what they said just as she had recorded the mouse's name.

Dick said: "Snow White scratched around in his cage." Jane added: "Snow White has pink eyes." Alice said: "He stood up on his hind legs and looked at us." And so on.

As each child offered an idea, the teacher wrote it, using appropriate manuscript writing and a heavy black crayola crayon. Pupils noted immediately that she could not write as fast as they talked. Even so, she wrote at a good pace and the waiting time was not long. After each idea had been recorded, she read it back to the group in general, and to the pupil dictating in particular. This is the way she proceeded, recording the ideas of six different pupils and completely filling the newsprint sheet. All this took but a few minutes, and the pupils were fascinated by the performance and were eagerly attentive. The account read as follows:

Snow White

Dick said, "Snow White
scratched around in his cage."
Jane said: "Snow White has pink
eyes." Alice said: "She stood up
on her hind legs and looked at
us." Jerry said: "Her tail is
two feet long." Bill said: "Snow
White ran around on the table."
Nancy said: "Snow White is soft
and furry."

Now the teacher read the entire story to the class. As she read, she pointed quickly and briefly to each word. Then all the class read the story together. The teacher pointed to each word as she proceeded, saying each word and the pupils saying it with her. Even though the pointing and the repeating after by the pupils made for some arhythm, a surprisingly even-paced performance resulted.

Next she gave each pupil an 8 x 11 inch sheet of white paper and asked them to make a drawing of Snow White. While the children were drawing she went about the room, writing the words *Snow White* at the top of each pupil's paper. She gave some a chance to show that they had already learned to copy writing as they proceeded to label their own paper.

Some of the things that had occurred as a result of this experience are as follows:

1. Pupils saw that reading was no more than talk written down.

2. They saw that the teacher could read back or play back all of the story or parts of it.

3. They followed the reading process on a left-to-right basis.

4. They made return sweeps from the end of one line on the right to the beginning of the next line on the left.

5. They saw that letters were made differently. Some few were capitals. *Snow White* always started with capital letters.

6. They saw the use of punctuation in a meaningful language context.

7. They experienced the thrill of "reading" as they read with the teacher.

8. Some of the pupils saw their names in writing and their ideas in writing.

9. They had displayed *curiosity,* as they watched and examined the mouse, and *creativity,* as they told about their reactions.

10. Oral language usage was stimulated as they reacted to seeing the mouse.

11. Ideas were shared in the dynamics of a class situation and in response to an immediate experience.

12. Teacher questions had caused them to observe more carefully.

13. Each had opportunities to listen to others speak, to hear their ideas, and to discover how others reacted to the same circumstances.

14. Each had an opportunity to vote and express preference for a name for the mouse and to learn how to accept the decision of the majority.

15. Each had an opportunity to make his own drawing and thus show the attributes about Snow White which he was reacting to and repro-ducing.

16. The name *Snow White* written on each illustration gave pupils an opportunity to link two symbols for the same referent: a printed name and a picture.

In addition, the teacher had an excellent opportunity to discover some things about her class:

1. their curiosity about the mouse;

2. their concern or lack of concern about seeing the mouse out of the cage and on the table, and their reluctance or readiness to touch the mouse;

3. their willingness to move about the table and among each other;

4. their oral language usage and, particularly, their choice of words;

5. their attention span, persistence, and cooperativeness;

6. whether some could read (as the story was being read back by the class, some few continued to run ahead and to do so correctly);

7. their ability to use crayons and to illustrate ideas (the illustrations were some index to maturity, and revealing in ways similar to the Goodenough Draw-A-Man Test).

For all concerned, this was a profitable experience. To be sure, the parents heard about the event. They also heard that reading had been done. "I read a story about Snow White," said one girl to her mother. "Oh," was the pleased reply. "You read about Snow White and the seven dwarfs?" "No, Mother, we read about a white mouse. We named him Snow White. See, here is his name on my pictures. He is standing up looking at us."

The next day this teacher divided the class into three groups on a random-order basis. In each group were two of the children who had dictated lines that were recorded in the Snow White chart. Then she had each group take a turn sitting with her in the back of the room and gathered about the chart of the previous day.

She started each group session by rereading the chart to them. Then they all reread it together as she pointed to the words. Next, she invited Jerry to stand by her and read the chart with her. She started by merely pointing to the name of the chart and Jerry immediately supplied *Snow White*. Each time the name Snow White appeared in the story, Jerry hurried ahead and read the words. He also recognized his name. "Reading" for Jerry had been a booming success.

Jane stood by the teacher next. Jane read the title, too, as did Jerry. However, each time the words Snow White appeared thereafter, Jane hesitated. All the teacher needed to do, though, in each instance was point to the same words in the title and Jane responded immediately. She, too, read her own name.

Others in the group were given opportunity to "read," too. The teacher stayed alert to the interest of the group and the activities of the rest of the class. Some were looking at books that had been placed on the library corner table. Others were in the house corner, playing. Still others were drawing. Some sat together; some preferred to work alone. The teacher was careful not to overplay the attention span and interest of the group sitting with her or of others in the class.

In the next group Nancy did a fine reading job. She read *Snow White* each time it appeared. She read the name of each pupil and the word *said*: "Dick said," "Jane said," and so on. When they got to the sentence she had dictated, she read all of it: "Nancy said, 'Snow White is soft and furry.'"

Dick took his turn and needed a little help with the story name. All the teacher did, though, was to make an s-s-s sound, and Dick caught on. This help was needed each time. A pause on his name was sufficient to prompt him to remember that this was his contribution and therefore his name.

In the third group Alice performed as Jerry had. Bill, however, astonished the group. He read almost the entire chart, needing help only with *scratched* and *furry*. Now the teacher went a step further. She asked Bill to locate certain words. First she said, "Point to your name." This he did quickly. Then she had him point to *Dick, Jane, Nancy, Jerry,* and *Alice* in that order. He found each name almost as quickly as he had located his own. Next she asked Bill to *count* the number of times *Snow White* appeared on the chart. He proceeded to count as he pointed, starting with the title, and gave the number five.

By this time the teacher had gathered the entire class around. Next she had Bill locate the words *table* and *around*. Both appeared in his contribution so she had felt reasonably confident about these two requests. Then she said, "One of those two words appears at some other place in the chart. Which one?" This was a challenging question. Bill needed to compare words and to make a decision. In a few seconds, though, he had located the word *around* in the second line.

Now the teacher tried one more thing. She saw that all this was holding the attention of the class. Also she realized that she was being given an ideal opportunity to make points about reading and how interesting it can be. She printed the word *table* on the chalkboard and asked Bill to read it. This he did instantly, even though it was in isolation. Then she wrote the number *two* on the board and he named it. Next she wrote the word *pink*. On his own Bill walked to the chart and found the word there, and then announced that the word was *pink*.

Many things occurred during this second go-around with the "Snow White" story that were very desirable from both a pupil and a teacher point of view. From a pupil point of view the following observations are particularly relevant.

1. Pupils had an opportunity to work in a group as well as to work on their own or with some other classmate.

2. When they were not in the reading group they had an opportunity to decide what they would do from a list of opportunities prescribed by the teacher.

3. They could do some "book selecting" at the library table.

4. They could read. As is evident by the detailed reports on the six dictators, the reading performance varied according to their ability to do so.

5. They could listen to others read.

6. Each pupil that had a chance to read had a chance to "succeed." Some read only the title but some, like Nancy, read six or more words.

7. The range of words read varied from Dick—who knew two words with a bit of hissing help from the teacher—to Bill who knew thirty-five of the thirty-seven different words and who read fifty-four of the fifty-six running words.

8. Visual discrimination of words was accomplished this early in the school year; and it was done without drawing shadow boxes—an extremely artificial crutch device at best.

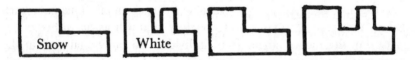

Neither did the teacher have to frame any of the words with her hands. This, too, is a weak sort of aid.

9. Visual-auditory discrimination occurred each time the pupils located in the story a word the teacher spoke and each time they read with her.

10. The sounds that letters represent were being linked on a phonetic word-attack basis, especially when the teacher helped Dick recall *Snow White* by making the s-s-s sound.

In many respects the teacher was able to do an informal inventory of readiness for reading. Each pupil's performance allowed her to make notes about skills possessed. For example, she now knew that Bill could read many words. He had already indicated that he knew thirty-five words.

This total is higher than that found in the first two preprimers of most series of readers. He knew words in isolation as well as in context. But above all, he knew how to use context clues to word meaning. When Bill returned to the chart to locate and identify the word *pink,* he showed awareness of one of the most important skills in a reader's word-attack repertoire—meaning clues.

On the other hand, Jerry indicated that he recognized three words: *Snow, White,* and *Jerry.* He knew *Snow White* each time it occurred in the chart, indicating clearly that he had a visual image for the word. It also indicated that he linked the right auditory image with the right visual image.

It is to be noted again that this stands in sharp contrast, not only to the content of preprimers, but also to the memoriter approach to word learning. This teacher did not give the class a list of words to take home so that distaste for reading could be reinforced at home as well as in school. Rather, she got their attention through an old "psychology of learning" trick. She used a *novel* experience, *different* and *vivid,* and within the children's grasp. Then she allowed the pupils to react by talking rather than by imposing her ideas. She arranged to have recontact or reinforcement of learning within twenty-four hours. It is during the first twenty-four hours that forgetting occurs at a rapid rate. This is true of logical as well as rote learning. Each time a pupil read the chart, others in the group had recontact with the words.

By the third day this teacher had reproduced the "Snow White" story on hectograph and had a copy available for each pupil. This gave each pupil an opportunity to pour over the story as much as he wished.

This day she moved about from individual to individual and in the private person-to-person session read through the story with each pupil. This time each word that a pupil could read in his own was underlined by the teacher. Some had only the title underlined, whereas Bill had every word underlined. In addition, the teacher wrote the name of each pupil at the end of the story. In a few instances pupils were able to write their own names.

On the library table was the story of *Snow White and the Seven Dwarfs.* Pupils gained a great deal of pleasure from the fact that they could read the words *Snow White* in a book. In addition, the teacher had a booklet about a snowman, and some pupils discovered they could read the word *snow* there, too. Some could read the entire word. One little girl brought with her from home a copy of *Jack and Jill* in which appeared a story with a winter setting. In the story the word *snow* was used a number of times.

So these children were encouraged to make a transfer of their reading knowledge immediately to different contexts. And, interestingly enough, they made the transfer without raising any questions about the differences in form and shape of the letters—print with different typeface styles and manuscript writing

In the meantime, the teacher accomplished all of the other getting-acquainted activities that are a part of a new class' first year in school: names and name cards, seats and desks, closets and the lavatory, the room and the teacher next door, the school nurse, the principal's office, and so on. She read to the children, told stories, had them listen to music, and soon had them settled into the business of school life.

Next Steps

Not all of the time was devoted to getting acquainted. Neither was all of the time devoted to reading. She did, however, continue with other experience stories of the "Snow White" type in which the pupils dictated in response to a shared and immediate firsthand experience. The school librarian stopped in one day and told a story to the class. This was used as a prop for pupil-dictated stories. A group of third grade level children stopped by one day and did a puppet show. This was an excellent source of stimulation.

After three weeks were completed this teacher had a good idea concerning the language facility, the interests and tastes, the intelligence, and the social-personal poise of each pupil. Now, in order to differentiate reading instruction and pace the learning of each on as nearly an individual basis as possible, she organized the class into four groups. The purpose for this organization was to permit teacher opportunity to obtain individually-dictated stories and to obtain enough of them to be useful. Moving around the room from pupil to pupil was not as efficient for systematic help as working out of smaller subgroups. The groups were roughly divided according to the four levels as described. Bill and five others were in a Level IV group. Nancy and seven others were in a Level III group. Jerry and eleven others were in a Level II group. And Dick and five others were in a Level I group.

In the Level IV group Bill was advanced well beyond the others. He already had a sizeable reading vocabulary and was having a grand time reading his way through the books in the library corner. This teacher with her modified individualized reading approach had made needed provisions for Bill and the other budding Bills. He was keeping his own record of books read and was sharing his enthusiasm and book knowledge with others in the room. This sharing he did informally on a friend-to-friend basis, a classmate-to-classmate basis; and already he had discovered that he could share on an interest-to-interest basis. Two others in his "dictating" group were catching on fast and doing a good deal of reading.

On the other hand, Dick and the pupils in his group seemed almost as if miles apart from Bill. Even so they were doing just what Bill was doing. They were dictating stories just as he was. Oftentimes they dictated about the same experience areas as he did. This was especially true when the interest source was one in which the whole class participated. They "read" their stories on the two-voice level. They read and that was the important thing! They got books on the library shelf and "read" them. Then, too, at times Bill would sit next to Dick in the library corner and in a low whisper read a story to him. Furthermore, at times Bill would help him with words when he was "re-reading" his old experience stories or reading a library book.

All in the class knew that Bill was just about the best reader, but all also knew that Dick was coming along. Dick knew this too. So did Dick's parents and so did Bill's parents. The climate that prevailed in the classroom was best clocked by the rising barometer measuring enthusiasm, good will, and self-reliance.

Once the class was organized into dictating groups, a teacher-group-contact cycle was developed. The plan drawn up permitted her to sit with each group to obtain pupil dictation on an average of two times a week. (This cycle will be enlarged upon later.) First, it seems timely to study carefully how the teacher worked with the Group IV people and the Group I people.

Group IV was Bill's group and had five members. At the appointed time the five pupils came to the dictating corner. The arrangement was such that pupils sat in a semicircle facing the teacher as the hub of the circle. This is how the group assembled and prepared for the individual story dictating session. In this instance the source of interest was a turtle that one of the boys had brought to school. Earlier in the day all of the children had gathered around to watch the turtle and to hear Bob tell how he found the turtle.

Now the turtle was in a box that looked like a suit box. Grass and twigs and a small rock were in the box as well as a pie tin with water. Stones were in the pie tin to help anchor it. The group was gathered about this exhibit, watching and talking.

The teacher then moved to the dictating table. This was a small table at pupil height. On it she had sheets of lined paper approximately 11 by 15 inches in size and a black crayola. A small screen was being used. This provided some privacy in that the pupil was screened from the group and the class. Then, one at a time, the pupils in the group took turns sitting with the teacher and dictating.

Bill sat down with the teacher and dictated the following story.

The Walking Fort

I called the turtle
"The Walking Fort" because
that is what he is. He
carries his fort on his back.
When he walks along, if
he sees some trouble, he
pulls in his neck and his
feet. Then he is safe in
his fort. I told my Dad
about the walking fort
and he said the turtle
was like an army tank.
But I like "The Walking
Fort" better.

After Bill had dictated the story, the teacher read it back to him to see if everything was in order. Bill said the story was right. Then the teacher gave the story to Bill, and he returned to his regular seat with it. There he could do a number of things with it. First, he reread the story. Bill was already so facile at learning new words that he was asked to underline only words he did not recognize or was not sure about. In this instance he could read the entire story. He paused at only the word *carries* but was able to recognize this word when he read on and got the meaning for the sentence. Even so, he drew a light wavy line under the word *carries*.

This done, he turned to his vocabulary book or new-word book as he called it. This was an alphabetized notebook. Bill's mother had bought it for him but he could have alphabetized it himself. He already knew the alphabet and could write many of the letters. The few he was not sure about he copied from the alphabet chart along the room wall. In this book he entered only words "new and interesting" to him. From this story he chose *turtle, fort, carries, trouble, neck, army, tank, better.*

While Bill was doing this, the other four members of the group were taking turns dictating. Edna, one of the four, dictated the following story.

Race

I could run a
race with the turtle.
He has four feet but
he can't go fast. I
have only two feet
but I could win
the race.

The story was read back to Edna and then she went to her seat. None in the group was as advanced as Bill. Even so, they were well enough along to underline only words they did not know or were not sure about. In this story Edna underlined *could, can't,* and *only.* Then she started to draw a picture to go with her story.

She had barely started with her picture when all in the group had finished dictating their stories. Then they all reassembled with the teacher and took turns reading their stories to each other. One at a time they came and stood by the teacher and reread the story orally. This procedure allowed the teacher to follow the oral reading and to note which words were underlined. So, she could be ready to supply the unrecognized words and thus help the oral reading and help the listener to get the story. In Edna's instance, she needed teacher help with *could* and *only.* As is often the case, the oral rereading of the story led to her recognition of the word *can't.* Somehow the demands of the oral reading, the language rhythm, and the flow of ideas seem to do the trick.

When the group meeting ended, all returned to their seats again. Bill continued with his vocabulary book. Edna and three others continued with their illustrations to accompany their stories.

At another time that day the teacher sat down with Dick's group of six. They, too, assembled around the turtle box and talked again about the turtle. Bob was in this group and he told again how the turtle came out of the water when his Dad was fishing. With this group the teacher did more perception prodding as the pupils watched the turtle move about in the box. She kept saying: "See how he pulls his head in;" "See how he goes around the rock;" and so on. Then she drew up the easel with a piece of newsprint thumbtacked on it. Then she recorded what the members of the group had to say. She used the "group" story approach with these pupils because they seemed in need of the intra-dependence thus obtained. They needed the stimulation of each other and got more of a story or an account than when they dictated alone. The account recorded in this instance was as follows.

Bob's Turtle

My Dad saw the
turtle when he fished.
The turtle is little.
The turtle can pull
his head in. He has
spots on his back.

Bob
Mae
Gale
Jimmy

The names on the end were those of the four pupils who gave sentences. The fact that not all contributed was of no concern. Some days all added an idea; some days only a few. Some days the group picked one member to tell the story for the group.

After the story was dictated the teacher read the story to the group, pointing to each word as she proceeded. Then different pupils took turns standing by the easel and reading the story together with the teacher. Bob was up first. He knew his own name and said the word *turtle* when he read the title. When they got to the word *turtle* in the first sentence he did not recognize it again. Instead of telling him the word immediately, the teacher pointed to the word in the title. Before he could answer, Jimmy popped up with the word. Bob knew the word *fished* when they got to it and he knew the word *turtle* the next two times it occurred.

Two more pupils read through the story with the teacher. Then the pupils returned to their seats to draw pictures to go with their story. They knew that by the next day the teacher would have reproduced a copy of the story for each. Bob drew a picture of his father fishing, Jimmy drew one to show the spots on the turtle's back, Dick drew a turtle on a rock, and so on.

By the time the teacher was through reading the story with the group, Bill had already read it from his seat as had Edna. Interest in reading and curiosity about what the others said prompted the action. And, of course, Bill was interested in how Dick was doing.

The next day the group of twelve—Jerry's group—met around the turtle box. On occasion, this group at this early stage dictated a group story as did Dick's group. However, whenever a story or account was dictated as a result of a firsthand experience, particularly one that could be examined and reexamined as this one could, individual stories were obtained.

A teacher concern usually voiced when a situation like this develops— taking twelve individual stories—is will there be time enough to do all this. Time should not be a factor and was not in this case. This does not mean that the concern voiced by such teachers is unfounded. The best answer is to show that it can be done and do so by firsthand demonstration. Of course, that is not possible in a text; but what is possible is to give an accurate account of a firsthand situation. That is what is being done here.

A demonstration with a comparable group was timed. The demonstration was performed in the Seaford, Delaware Central Elementary School and was observed by five other teachers. The presence of the other teachers added some extraneous factors that might have interfered with the progress of the demonstration, but it did not.

The group was assembled and the interest area briefly discussed with the pupils. Ideas were shared, and thinking was stimulated. Then one at a time the pupils sat down with the teacher and dictated their accounts.

The stories were recorded as previously described for the Group IV people. None of the stories were over three sentences. This occurred late in September of the school year and, while the pupils already had experience dictating stories and expressing their own ideas, they were neither that verbose nor that creative to give more. Each, though, had his own ideas and voiced them in his own, individual way.

After each child had dictated his version, he returned to his seat and reread the story. As he reread he *underlined* with a single black line *each word he* felt he *knew*. Guesses were not to be underlined—only words they felt sure about.

When all had dictated their stories and the last one had had a few minutes to reread and mark his story, all reassembled in the dictating area. There, one by one, they read their story version to the group. The teacher clipped each child's story on the easel at pupil-eye-level height. Then the teacher and the pupil read the story together. The teacher pointed to each word as she proceeded and allowed for enough hesitation to encourage the child to say the word if he knew it or thought he did. Again, as with the Group I pupils, oftentimes the language pattern and the on-goingness of the idea helped the pupil recall and speak words that he would otherwise not know on his own.

The time for this whole procedure was thirty-three minutes. Twenty-three minutes were used in the dictating and recording phase, and ten minutes in the oral rereading and sharing phase. The whole procedure was unhurried, nevertheless.

Some typical stories are as follows:

Mr. Turtle
Mr. *Turtle* walks on
four feet. He is very slow.

The Funny House
The turtle walks
around in his *house*. His
house has a hard roof. It's
a funny house.

Spotty
The *turtle* has
spots like my *cat*. I
called him *Spotty*. That's
my cat's name.

The Turtle
When *the turtle* eats
he sticks his head out.
His *eyes* are open.

Slow and Easy
I like a *turtle.*
I like to watch him
crawl around. *He is*
slow and easy.

The words underlined are those the pupils felt they knew when they reread their stories at their seats. Underlining known words is a positive approach to word learning. The emphasis is on what is known. It also calls for a facing up to the facts; either one knows or does not know or guesses. So the act requires a certain amount of intellectual honesty. The need to "prove knowledge" occurs when the oral reading is done. The teacher will pause a bit longer on each underlined word. If the word is unrecognized the teacher supplies the word and the underlining is marked: —|—|—|—|—|—|—|—|—|—|—|—.

All this done the pupils are now ready to prepare a picture of a turtle or a turtle scene. Pictures of turtles may be available in old magazines. If expendable, the pictures may be cut out and used instead of a pupil drawing.

Next, the Level III group, or Nancy's group, was assembled. All eight gathered around the turtle to watch and talk and share ideas. Then one by one they sat down with the teacher and dictated their accounts of their turtle observations and their ideas. Some of the accounts were similar, in length and originality, to those dictated by members of Bill's group; others were more like the Level II group accounts. Nancy dictated the following:

> *The Lonesome Turtle*
> *I believe* the turtle
> is lonesome. He *walks*
> *around so slow* and
> looks *so sad. Sometimes*
> he looks out *at us* and
> then he *pulls his head*
> in *again. I believe*
> he is lonesome.

Nancy returned to her seat and underlined words she did not know or was not sure about. Nancy was a cautious person—more inclined to underestimate her knowledge than to overestimate it. The underlined words reflect these conditions.

Nancy's reaction to the turtle also reflects her personal dispositions[1] and motives. Her style of response to the turtle suggests a servicing of a strong, compelling motive for the regard for the welfare of others. The sensory cue of the one little turtle in the big box being watched by many, and poking his head out and pulling it in again, apparently was sufficient to arouse this flow of ideas. Nancy's general disposition finds many stimuli

---

[1]Allport, Gordon W. *Pattern and Growth in Personality*. New York: Holt, Rinehart & Winston, 1961.

that are functionally equivalent and guide her to a form of behavior that
already is being labeled as: "That's Nancy for you." This is not only
Nancy's way of reacting to her environment but her way of meeting it.

At the risk of being repetitious, this seems like an opportune time to
repeat Samuel Johnson's counsel implied in the statement: "Speak so that
I may see you."[2] Every dictated story gives pupils an opportunity to speak
and to "show" themselves. Similarly, every dictated story or account gives
teachers an opportunity to "see" pupils' essential characteristics, because
dispositions are in continuous flow. "Interests, ambitions, compulsions,
phobias, general attitudes, inclinations, hobbies, values, tastes, predilections—all are personal dispositions (some only secondary) and are at the
same time motives."[3]

Rick dictated the following story and revealed personal dispositions of
his.

The Explorer

This turtle is an
explorer. He *goes*
around exploring. He
came out of the
water to explore.
He explores *our* box.

Word Banks

On this second day the teacher also met again with the Level IV and
Level I groups. The Level IV people used the group assembly for a dual
purpose. First it served as a waiting pool as each took turns sitting with the
teacher and reading again their dictated turtle accounts. Bill recognized
the only word he had been uncertain about—*carries.* He had brought with
him to this private conference his New Word Book and indicated that he
had entered the word *carries.* Edna also recognized the three words she
had underlined: *could, only, can't.* Now the teacher performed another
interesting job. She carefully printed these three words on small rectangular-
shaped pieces of substantial white paper. Each piece was approximately
⅜ths of an inch wide and 1½ inches long. Putting the words on these
small cards gave each pupil a private file of words.

The private file served any number of purposes. Foremost on this list

---

[2]Johnson, Samuel. Attributed to.

[3]Allport, *op. cit.,* p. 373.

was the opportunity it provided the children to manipulate the words on their desk tops. The words could be used to produce stories or accounts of their own choosing. This is an especially effective way to get children to use and reuse these words and to do so with a purpose—a purpose they wanted to accomplish.

Using a Pupil Word Card Holder* they could perform with ease. A Word Card Holder provides a surface upon which pupils may place words. A slight pressure will make each word adhere to the surface until the pupil wishes to remove it again. The holder may be placed either horizontally or vertically and cards may be lined up in straight lines by placing them on the impressed rules.

Peggy, a member of the Level III dictating group, had set up the following story on her Word Card Holder.

PETS

I	like	pets	.

The	Turtle	is

a	pet	in	our

room	.	Do	You

like	pets	?

Peggy

Even though each word had been placed on a ⅜ths inch by 1½ inch card, Peggy—as did all the other children—cut the cards down to the size of the words: | I | | I | ; | the | | the |

Placing the words on a Holder had many advantages. First, the fact that the cards adhered to the surface meant that they stayed in place. Second, the Holder could be moved about easily without upsetting the word arrangement. Third, pupils could swap Holders and thus exchange stories. Fourth, the words could be removed with ease and refiled for future use.

---

*Pupil Word Card Holder. Winston Communications Program. New York City: Holt, Rinehart & Winston, Inc.

Pupils could write notes to each other. Edna wrote a note to Patsy.

| May | I | read | your | turtle | story | ? |

Patsy put the answer on her Holder: | Yes | . |

While the teacher was working with the Level III group, Dick with the help of Bill put this question on his Holder: | May | I | use |

| the | easel | to | paint | my | picture | ? | At this stage Dick could read only three words in that question: | May | I |

| picture | but he knew what the question asked. Even though the teacher was busy in a private pupil conference, Dick walked up to her and waited quietly until she could turn to him. Then he handed his Holder to her. She read the message, added the word | yes | , and returned the Holder to him. This communicating act took but a few seconds and did not disturb the room. Dick had waited quietly until the teacher had acknowledged his presence. This was communicating with a purpose.

Pupils could play word-matching games. Joanna and Frances did a visual discrimination word-matching game. Joanna put the word | turtle | on her board and Frances put the same word on her board. Then Frances put up the word | the | and Joanna matched it.

Carl and Ray did an initial consonant visual discrimination matching. Carl put the word | ball | on his board and Ray put up a word that began with the same letter, b: | boy | . Then he put up | stop | and Ray put up | stone | .

Jean and Ed were working together doing a very timely auditory-visual discrimination word-matching based on initial single consonants and consonant blends. Jean in a low whisper pronounced a word and Ed had to find a word in his file that had the same beginning sound. Jean said the word | table | . Ed found the word | turtle | in his file and put it on his Holder for Jean to see.

If in the process of writing a Holder story a pupil needed to use a word not yet in his file box, he turned to the teacher and had her put the word on a card. For example, Jerry wanted to use the word *running* so the teacher put it on a card for him: | running | . This word was not added to Jerry's vocabulary notebook until he could recognize it at any time, anywhere.

All in all, this Pupil Word Card Holder rendered a considerable service. Teachers are always looking about for activities that pupils can do on their own while they are busy with a pupil or a group. The activities described here in this discussion of the Holder kept many children on the go. Not only were they occupied, they were fruitfully occupied. These pupils were busy creating, assembling ideas, manipulating words, increasing their reading vocabularies, fixing more permanently retention of words previously learned, refining word-attack skills (both phonetic analysis and structural analysis skills), teaming up and working together, sharing, and so on. One other factor was also true—the room was astonishingly quiet. These six-year-olds were busily engaged in reading activities in which they were interested and which they could do.

The other half of the dual purpose of the second-day gathering of Level IV pupils was the swapping of stories. Pupils loved this part of the get-together even more than the pupil-teacher visit. Not only was it a pleasure and a privilege to read someone else's story, but also it was gratifying and inspiring to have someone else read your story. Pride of authorship is stimulating and ego building. These children were not only budding readers but also budding authors. Language arts were truly communication arts.

When the Level I dictating group reassembled on the second day, the group chart was made available. Then, one by one each member of the group took a turn "reading" the story orally. Again, each child stood by the teacher and followed her voice as they read the story together. Today, though, one *big* item was different. The pupil had the pointer and pointed from word to word as the story was read. Another big difference was observable. The teacher adjusted her voice and her rate of reading in such a toned-down way that much initiative rested with the pupil. In some instances a pupil literally took over and read ahead. This teacher was acting much as a swimming instructor does on occasion. Gradually as the person is paddling along, the instructor withdraws his support and almost without realizing it the learner swims along on his own.

After each had read the story orally the teacher moved a step further. She pointed to words (note—she did not cup the words in her hand) and asked pupils to name them. Dick knew twelve of the words: *turtle*, appearing four times, *Bob, Dad, fished, in, back, spots, little, in.* Next the teacher covered the chart and wrote certain words on the board in isolation. Everyone recognized *turtle* in isolation. Four knew *Bob's* name. One knew *fished*. Three knew *Spots*. Five knew *little*, and so on. Each word a pupil knew in isolation was placed on one of the small cards. Again the pupils in the Level I group were "doing" all the things being done in the Level IV group.

Now the teacher and the Level I people went to the library table. There they found the word *turtle* in the title of a book. They also found the word in different pages in the book. Then they turned to an encyclopedia and found the word *turtle* in the index. The teacher then turned to the right page in the volume by using the page number shown in the index. Why did she do this? By so doing even the Level I pupils could, when on their own, pick up an encyclopedia volume and turn to the section on *turtles* and enjoy the pictures. This was building the "encyclopedia habit" from the very beginning of the educational career of these budding scholars.

Also during this *turtle* week, pupils brought in magazine items and newspaper clippings about turtles. The interest in turtles and words spilled over into the after-school hours. This happened not because the teacher sent home a list of *turtle* words to be memorized but because these children were interested. Again this circumstance is a far cry from what happens all too often. Thank goodness there was no anxiety and fear—only eagerness and pleasure. The thirty-one pupils in this room had no need to pull in their reading necks behind a protective shutting-out shell.

At the end of the *turtle* go-around, when the Level II and III pupils had had their second day and the Level I pupils had had a third day, all the stories were clasped together and placed on the Pupil Story File. This teacher used wire clothes hangers with skirt-holding clips attached. The stories were all clipped as a stapled package to the clothes hanger and hung on a story birch rod. Now pupils could go to the story rod any time they were free to do so and take down the *turtle* stories. As the year progressed the story birch rod filled up and pupils had a catalogue of their own creations all packaged together. It was fun, even in November, to go back and select the *turtle* file and reread the stories and reminisce about the long ago week with the turtle. In addition, pupils could readily see what progress they had made in learning to read. By November even more pupils can read all of the stories suspended from the turtle hangers on the story birch rod. Here was a teacher who did not believe in "sparing the rod and spoiling the child."

The *turtle* stories were told in response to a firsthand experience situation. All had seen the turtle, examined him, and talked about him. Dictating an account or a story about him prompted the use of vocabulary known to each pupil.

Picture stories: Stories can be motivated by using a picture or pictures. Reading readiness books lend themselves well for such use, as do big pictures frequently a part of a readiness program. Some big pictures are planned to be used primarily as a source of inspiration for dictated stories (Harry Sartain's, Language Arts Charts, D. C. Heath & Company). A three- or four-episode story told in three or four pictures helps some children see how ideas are related. Some may dictate one idea about each picture or three or four pupils may be involved, each telling about one picture in the sequence.

There is also the opportunity to extend experience even at the picture level. Certainly using pictures is not as good a way to do this as is a firsthand experience basis; but it is a way that children, even at age six, have used many times. Certainly, too, it is true that they will use this approach many more times in their educational life. Pictures or illustrations are the only way to get into history and, in many instances, to move about geographically. So, the use of a picture can serve worthwhile purposes.

Telling a story in response to a picture is different from the relating that can be done in telling about a firsthand experience. The picture prop requires the pupils to project from their experiences a plot or schemata that does not really exist. Of course, the elements in the pictures do suggest some intra-relationship; however, *what, how, why, who, where, when* is largely up to the projector.

When the parts have been dictated, they can be linked together by a main title and subtitles. Even though some children find this idea rather challenging, they can usually think of a name.

A dictating cycle was set up by a teacher and flexibly followed. Roughly, it was a plan to meet with two groups on one day to record a story and with the other two groups on the next day. On the second day the teacher met again with the two groups started on the first day to give them an opportunity to reread their stories and check on word retention after twenty-four hours.

This phase of the working cycle might be charted as follows:

DICTATING GROUPS SCHEDULE

	Mon.	Tues.	Wed.	Thurs.	Fri.
Level I	dictate story	reread story word study	reread story word study	dictate story	reread story word study
Level II	other activities	dictate story	reread story word study	reread story word study	dictate story
Level III	other activities	dictate story	reread story word study	other activities	dictate story
Level IV	dictate story	reread story word study	other activities	dictate story	reread story word study

This plan could be adapted as circumstances warranted. On occasion, the Levels I and II groups did not have a second rereading day. On occasion, activities related to a single experience area and a single chart or set of charts require the five days of the school week. Sometimes, too, the Levels III and IV groups needed a second rereading day. Of course, it must be kept in mind that the levels, as charted here, represent groups of children grouped because of the results obtained on the Informal Reading Readiness Test and the Standardized Reading Readiness Test. Thus the Level IV group was most mature and the Level I group least mature.

How to keep the cycle going should not prove a problem. The world is so full with so many wonderful things that it abounds like a well-stocked stream with many, many areas of interest. Children, like adults, like to talk about themselves, their possessions, their home, their family, their pets, their friends, their neighbors, their relatives, their trips. The question is not so much *what* to talk about as it is a matter of selecting. In addition, the special events in the school year, as well as the holidays, provide innumerable diamonds: school days, festivals, assemblies, visitors, playground, Halloween, Thanksgiving, Christmas, Lincoln's birthday, Valentine's Day, Washington's birthday, Easter. All of this, along with a readiness book or two, provides a larder full and overflowing.

This teacher prepared a guide-plan of interest areas that could be used for a month or more. She listed four areas per week, even though she knew that most likely only two would be used. In addition she allowed for the rich incidental and unexpected events, such as Bobby's lost tooth, Dolores' pet's baby kittens, the welcome home extended a local boy who was a World Series hero, the crash of an abandoned aircraft into a local lumber yard. The teacher's guide gave the comfort that she sought in regard to interest areas. She knew that she would never exhaust the opportunities. She also knew that field trips could be quite useful if wisely planned. Trips could also be time consuming and yield few returns.

Structured Units: In addition the teacher used the multitude of ideas available and structured in an American English program planned for use at the first grade level (*American English Book I,* Burrows, Stauffer, Vasquez, Holt, Rinehart & Winston, 1960). The sequence of contents dealt with social studies, science, arithmetic, weather, art, and human relations. Many selections of verse were included also. Some are gay, some are serious; some are short, some are longer; some are about familiar things, and some are about faraway things. Every child should have some contact with verse which seems just right to him.

Earlier herein it was suggested that the answer to the number of charts to obtain was "a million." Of course, this is an exaggeration but a positively slanted one. Implicit, though, in the idea of many charts is another thought that plagues many an unknowing teacher who tries "experience charts" without fully appreciating their value and usefulness. As a result, these unwitting teachers get a class "dictated" experience chart and use it as they would a preprimer.

They go over and over the chart day after day trying to get the children to memorize the words in the chart. Eventually they discover that this use of an "experience" chart is no better than the preprimer approach.

Individual, group, and class charts are to be obtained. Each type serves a purpose, and its use should be determined by the purpose served. On a quantity basis alone, individual charts will yield by far the largest number. As already indicated, in the classroom circumstances described, individual charts were obtained with three of the levels: Groups II, III, and IV. Group charts were obtained with the Level I group.

Individual charts permit and encourage each pupil to use his own words to express his ideas. It is this "mine" feature that makes individual charts a veritable gold mine. Not only can they reflect a pupil's language facility but also his own curiosity, interests, and creativity. In this respect they are as useful as they are for word usage. Reexamine the charts already presented in this text and note how each of these factors is in evidence.

Even though the same interest area, *turtles,* was used to motivate chart dictation, the words used reflect individual preferences and differences. When Bill's account is compared with Edna's account, the differences are well illustrated. Bill used forty different words, and Edna used twenty; and only six words are common to both (*I, the, turtle, he, feet, but*). The differences are equally as striking when the five accounts dictated by five members of Level II group are examined. Now one might conclude that because the accounts are short and were dictated by less fluent pupils, the number of common words would be considerable. Quite to the contrary, only *one word* is common to all five stories, and that is the word *turtle*—the interest area around which all stories are built. The number of different words in each is as follows: ten words; thirteen words; fourteen words, thirteen words; and fourteen words. A comparison of the titles gives a ready indication of interest differences: "Mr. Turtle," "The

Funny House," "Spotty," "The Turtle," and "Slow and Easy." Creativity is apparent in the titles but even more so in the content account.

Individual charts encourage the same kind of creative freedom in choice of pupil illustrations. What to illustrate and how is determined by each pupil.

Individual charts permit and encourage the exchange of charts. As chart after chart is accumulated, a rich chart library is being built. Children love to go to the chart library and choose a chart or a set of charts to read. In this case it is doubly exciting to select and read because all authors are known. Each is a celebrity in his own right.

Individual charts can be reproduced and swapped. "I'll give you a copy of my *turtle* chart for a copy of your Post Office chart," said one pupil to another, and so on.

Individual charts fit well into a personal chart notebook or folder. Each pupil can be provided with a chart notebook in which he staples or pastes all of his charts. This gives him a running inventory of his own progress. Each chart is dated as it is entered, and at the end of the year each has a fine chart chronology. These notebooks should be substantial enough to survive an occasional taking home.

Group charts are particularly useful in a group situation like the one Dick was a member of, Level I. At the early stage in their first-grade careers, for various and sundry reasons, Dick and others like him had difficulty telling a story or giving an account, and doing so on their own. Jointly, however, they did reasonably well. The dynamics of a joint effort are enough to carry it through.

An excellent approach with a group situation is to proceed as the pupils did in the following illustration. Five of the children in a first grade rolled a snowman at recess time. Back indoors after recess the five were assembled to dictate an account of the snowman rolling. The five pupils were not all in the same level groups. This was a friendship group. The pupils sat together for a few minutes and reviewed with each other what they had done. Then they chose one of the group to be spokesman for the group and tell "their" story. In this instance they selected a little fellow who had missed a good bit of school and was, as a result, being a bit reluctant to talk up at other times. This little fellow sat with the teacher and told what happened. The other four sat listening with the eager sympathy of mother hens watching their chick try his wings. When he faltered at one point, one of the group gave him a hint and on he went. After the story had been recorded, the pupil who dictated read through the story with the teacher and did an astonishing job. He did not let his friends down. Then the others took turns reading the story orally.

Class charts can in some ways be used in much the same way that group charts are used. It must be kept in mind that the increased number of participants also multiplies the number of difficulties. Class charts are more often of the directive type: a class chart on how to conduct oneself on a school bus; what to do when an unknown word is encountered while reading a book selected in the library; a weekly class plan chart; how to watch a TV show; how to keep weather records, and so on.

Word Banks

There is a change of climate in the first grade classrooms where the vocabulary winds shift direction to the development of a personalized word bank based on sound investments. Removed are peak-and-valley forgetting periods created by continuous effort at memorizing a fixed word list. Excessive word memorization has been categorized by experience as an exercise in futility. On the other hand, those who refuse to indulge in petty word-parroting goals advocate the accumulation of a seasoned vocabulary filled with meaning and logical association aids to recall.

Every individually-dictated story represents a personalized word usage record. In the eyes of the pupil the words in his chart are: "My words in writing." Possession may be recognized as nine points of the law but also, in word learning, as nine points of retention.

Every time a pupil marks a word in his chart as a known word he is underlining the "my spoken word—my printed word" idea. In a way he is awarding himself his own gold star. Each underlined word in the stories represents a pupil-recognized achievement. He knew the word and he drew the line. Should he forget the word—as he may do, being human and not infallible—his total story, plus his picture or illustration, provide many meaningful clues to re-recognition.

These words, as stated earlier, are put on small word cards (⅜ inch by 1½ inches) by the teacher and put into one of the child's word banks. The cards may be kept in a word box for ready use on a Pupil Word Card Holder. When eight or ten words have been accumulated, the pupil begins to see the need for putting the words in some order. This is the time to set up an alphabetized word bank box. For this purpose, one pupil brought to school an egg box which, when opened up, had twenty-four compartments. Each compartment was indexed with a letter of the alphabet, except that the last one was marked X, Y, Z. Now the words he had accumulated could be filed alphabetically and thus make them more readily available for use. Another child brought a box that had been used to house small Christmas balls. Some children used small envelopes labelled alphabetically and assembled in a box. Various types of "boxes" can be used. The important thing is the experience of filing words by alphabet—requiring the giving of attention to the initial letter of a word and requiring the pupil to deal with and learn the use of the alphabet in a very practical and meaningful way.

Some children put each word on the top line of a three-by-five card, and then filed the cards in a box by alphabetical order. On the card they put the name of the story in which the word was first underlined and the sentence from the story in which the word was first used. Whenever possible, they illustrated the word or found a small picture that could be cut out and pasted on the card, thus assembling in a sense their own picture dictionary. In addition, when circumstances permitted, the pupil found the word in other places such as newspapers, old magazines, and very old books; cut the word out; and pasted it on the card. They could also copy a sentence from someone else's chart or from a book on the library table. All of this provided highly-to-be-endorsed busy work.

Other children put their words into a word-bank notebook. One girl brought a notebook to which she and an older sister had attached alphabet indexing stickers. Most of the notebook users labeled pages alphabetically by hand. Notebooks were easier to handle in many ways and could be taken home. In addition, they looked like private dictionaries. These pupils also copied a "first use" sentence and found other uses in other sources. Pupils soon discovered, though, that card users had an advantage in that they could alphabetize words that began with the same letters, i.e. *about, along, an, army*. Words recorded in a notebook did not allow for this unless a great deal of erasing and rearranging was done.

These word banks provided the security of a sound investment. The account could be drawn on at any time without depleting the principal. Pupils could draw on the account when using the Pupil Word Card Holder; when doing word-recognition activities, either under teacher direction or in collaboration with another pupil; and especially when doing creative writing and faced with a spelling need. The interest on each word investment in the word bank far exceeded anything available on the world economic scene.

Furthermore, the "dictionary" habit was being built into the pupils' stock of learning habits. Moving from their own dictionaries, with their alphabetized arrangement and illustrative sentences, to picture dictionaries, to standard dictionaries could be accomplished by easy stages.

Word Recognition Training

The experience story or modified individualized reading approach provides innumerable top priority opportunities to teach word-attack skills. Every story recorded and witnessed by the pupils has provided visual discrimination and auditory discrimination opportunity. Children can see each spoken word become a printed word. They see each letter being formed. They note differences in letter configuration and word configuration. Some letters extend above a line and some below: *b, d, f, h, k, l, t,* and *g, j, p, q, y, z.* Some are on the line only: *a, c, e i m n, o, r, s, u, v, w, x.* Some words are long; some are short: *flooded, in.* Some look very much alike: *in, on, an, no.* All of this they learn to "see" as they watch chart after chart being prepared, and as they "read" through chart after chart with the teacher. And all of this is learned without pressure to memorize and is done in a very functional setting— the recording and rereading of stories. There is nothing artificial or stilted or forced about all of this. To the contrary, it is meaningful, continuous, and paced. It is as Boney so aptly put it: "learning to read as they learned to talk."[4] It is a learning to deal with printed words in a real, live communication circumstance.

Gradually, and often quite quickly, pupils begin to discriminate words. When they find how often a word appears on a chart as described earlier, selective and purposeful word discrimination is being done of both a visual and an auditory nature. And both acts are done in conjunction with a reading act, and are not divorced from it as is done when such skills are being jammed in isolation.

Once words are recognized, they can be used to teach specific word-attack skills selectively. The moment a child can read *one* word, this can be started. For example, a child who can read only his name can be asked to decide whether another name begins or ends in the same way as his does. This can be done either by sight or by sound.

When *Dick* can read his name, the teacher can ask him to decide whether or not the name she says begins like his name. For this she can

---

[4]Boney, C. DeWitt. "Teaching Children to Read as They Learned to Talk," *Elementary English Review,* XVI, No. 4 (April 1939), pp. 139-141, 156.

use other names like *David, Bill, Darlene, Nancy,* and so on. She can also print these same names on the board or on paper and ask him to underline each name that begins with the same letter as his name: *Dick —David, Darlene.*

When Dick can read two or more words, the complexity of the demands and the decision making can be increased. Now the teacher confronts Dick with the two words he knows: *Dick* and *turtle.* She says: "I am going to say a word that begins like one of these two words. Point to the right word." Then she pronounces words like *desk, table, door, down, toy, ten.* Note that the spoken word always fits one or the other circumstance. The same can be done visually. Also, similar practices can be initiated with inflectional changes and derivatives: *walk, walking; run, runs; fly, flying; carry, carries.* The opportunities for such activities are legion.

Filing the words or preparing a word dictionary requires further attentiveness to word structure. Not only are single letter beginnings dealt with but also letter combinations when filing such *blends* and *dipthongs* as *black, she, the, tree.* Now the letters in the alphabet take on functional significance as they are used to put words in order. The filing allows pupils to deal with these situations in circumstances that are rich with meaning and bristling with purpose. *Letter names* serve a real purpose which is different from *letter sounds.*

They All Want to Write

They All Want To Write[5] is the title of an inspiring, sound, and far-reaching book done in the late thirties by a group of teachers who were practicing what they were preaching. Even though the book has been revised and reissued since 1939, the philosophy and methodology is the same. It is the kind of book all elementary school teachers should own and all first grade level teachers should have on their desks ready for constant use. As the title suggests, it is a book on creative writing and, as Paul Witty says in his Foreword to the book: ". . . this volume brings out . . . the fact that creative writing offers an excellent vehicle for recognizing, respecting, and cultivating individuality."[6]

One of the hardest worked words in educational circles is the word *functional*—everything has to serve a function, and rightly so. To be

---

[5]Burrows, Alvina Treut, June D. Ferebee, Doris C. Jackson, and Dorothy O. Saunders. *They All Want to Write.* New York: Prentice-Hall, Inc., 1952.
[6]Ibid., p. vii.

functional something has to serve a purpose and have utility value for the
user. Thus, functional spelling represents the skill needed to spell while
one is writing a letter or a report or a paper or a book. A principal value
of creative writing is that it invariably is functional writing: stories,
accounts, notes, letters, posters, advertisements, book records, word files,
and so on. These kinds of writing activities can serve pupil purposes
without being drummed-up by a teacher. If children's writing is done to
the accompaniment of the steady tum-tum beat of contrived teacher-
copying acts, pupils quickly develop that veiled look of whipped attention
and the over-exaggerated cackle of drummed-up enthusiasm that can ring
so hauntingly in one's ears. Sure the children are laughing, but . . . ?

Early writing experiences[7] involve writing a name, notes to a teacher,
to home; get-well letters; birthday letters; permission for trips; thank-you
notes; invitations; telling and writing about Fall; about the weather; and
so on. At first, copying is hard work and requires much elbow room—big
pencils and big paper. Control and improvement is brought on quickest by
the need to communicate. If someone has to read your writing, and a
hoped-for answer is dependent upon their reading it, motivation soars
rapidly. This is true even if the "hoped-for answer" is *only* a word of
praise. Children need to be encouraged and helped. Expectancies must be
adjusted to individual differences in writing, just as they must in all skills
of life. Handwriting experts and fortune tellers can distinguish one handwriting from another, and thank goodness that the concept of individual
differences in handwriting has spread into handwriting classes. Legibility,
yes, but not goose-quilted uniformity.

Gradually children acquire writing skills that enable them to write their
own stories as well as dictate them. Written stories or notes or accounts
take more time and usually are shorter than dictated accounts. But this is
not a liability of written stories, but rather an asset of dictated accounts.
In fact, during the early writing days a teacher may step in and rescue a
piece of writing by writing the end for the pupil.[8]

Without a doubt pupils cannot spell all the words they want to use,
but the remarkable thing about their spelling attempts is the degree of
accuracy it represents—phonetic accuracy. The following examples illustrate this. The astonishing phonetic accuracy of children who want to
write and are encouraged to do so is evidence again—if more is needed—
that children who have learned to talk do have an ear for sound and that

[7]Burrows, Alvina T., and Russell G. Stauffer. *American English,* Book I.
[8]Burrows, *et al., op. cit.*

phonetics cannot be the monster of rules and regulations, even the augmented monster it is made out to be, or else children would not fare so well on their own. Illustrative are the following:

clinb	for	climb	cilled	for	killed
dag	"	dog	stared	"	started
geting	"	getting	astonot	"	astronaut
Monaday	"	Monday	likeed	"	liked
Autumu	"	Autumn	fends	"	friends
skaed	"	scared	astronoutnot	"	astronaut
woching	"	watching	hose	"	house
dansing	"	dancing	floteing	"	floating

My Maknet*

This is my maknet
(magnet)
fishing. My mother is
woching me. And so is
(watching)
my sister.

Jean

The Big Storm*

Five of the children
dice. That was very, very bad.
No one like it.

The Storm*

Pets do not like
the wind. It was floded.
Houses were floteing.
And Pets and People
were sat.

Any stories taken home by a pupil must be rewritten and the words must be correctly spelled. Pupils accept this standard and see why it should be adopted. Thus, at this early stage children can learn the value of a first

*Stories with an asterisk were made available to this author by three teachers in the West Seaford Elementary School, Seaford, Delaware.

draft, and a second draft, and a final copy. This is a practice many college students have not acquired nor learned to appreciate.

Burrows *et al.* say this:

We value highly those situations through which we can lead children to care enough about what they are composing to give it a personal flavor. We believe that if a child is to grow in power in written language, he must learn early to respect his individual way of saying things.[9]

Then they go on to describe a working file of unfinished and unpolished papers that was kept in the room at a place where the papers were readily accessible to all. This meant, of course, that visitors could see it, too. So it was decided that some label was needed to alert visitors to the fact that the file housed unfinished manuscripts. Suggested was a title: "Work Under Way." This represents a sound and realistic approach to written communication and to the need for standards.

In short, then, pupils do want to write. It is the wise teacher who takes full advantage of this natural desire. It represents an excellent way to make the communication arts become the integrated arts. As for initial reading instruction, it is a wonderful way to bring to communication the exactness and accurateness that Bacon said would result from writing.

In Summary

It has been said that while one may trust a man's probity one may not likewise trust his predilections. Predilection implies a strong liking that results from one's temperament, one's principles, or one's previous experience, and that predisposes one to prefer certain kinds of friends, or books, or methods, or to accept a thing without reference to any other test.[10] If there is any leaning apparent in this chapter, it is toward a good start in the educational life of everyone.

The temper of the tempered statements should clearly reflect the amount of strong feeling involved. The principles should clearly reflect a belief in the fact that learning to read can be accomplished with the same communication effectiveness and motivation as was learning to talk; that memorization is no substitute for understanding; that repeating facts is no substitute for reflective thought; and that permanent reading habits are not acquired in the quicksand of gold stars or scarlet letters. Experience as a teacher, a clinician, a consultant has fostered the conclusion that all of

[9]Burrows *et al., op. cit.,* p. 24.
[10]*Webster's Dictionary of Synonyms.* Springfield, Mass.: G. & C. Merriam Co., 1942.

our children bring with them "excellent bread, meat, and wine to the Inn in Trochate," which resource can be converted into an unprecedented literacy. It is a pity that in the midst of such potentialities one finds Procrustean famines. Resources are not the problem. The difficulty is man. The contraceptive methods of lock-step teaching and rote-memorization learning need to be replaced with the art of personalized discovery and reflective thought. Initial reading instruction is one area in which we can get "off the beach."

JOHN C. MANNING

FRESNO STATE COLLEGE

8. Early Letter Emphasis Approaches

OF THE HIGHER MENTAL PROCESSES, the search for classification models which provide order, sequence, and system for accumulated information, uniquely impels both the sciences and the arts to more refined levels of scholarly achievement and practical application.

Among the giants of human thought who have dominated the progress of Western man, three exceed all measure of excellence. Each contributed, for his age and for the ages which followed, those unifying principles of scientific classification which structure order from conflict and allow accommodation in variance.

The first of these intellectuals, the Greek Aristotle, classified the sciences, perhaps for all time, into three exclusive categories: Theoretical and speculative philosophy, practical philosophy, and productive philosophy. Applying the syllogism frame and deductive reasoning, Aristotle was able to compromise a world of the senses as described by Socrates, with a world of the spirit as defined by Plato.

The Middle Ages were illuminated by the genius of Thomas Aquinas who, like Aristotle before him, was able to draw a distinction between the actual and potential. Perhaps as few others before him and certainly fewer after him, Aquinas utilized his capacities of analysis, synthesis, and construction to formulate a philosophical base upon which the morals and ethics of Western man have depended since that point in time.

The classic principle of Aquinas, "Seldom affirm, never deny, always distinguish," has efficiently served scholars through the ages in their search for universal truths.

The Renaissance Natural Science movement reached its culmination with the publication of Darwin's brilliant *Origin of the Species.* Applying principles of detailed observation and classification, Darwin developed a science of comparative anatomy which proved compatible with paleontological history and man's desire to know of his beginnings.

119

To the degree that each of these intellectuals was able to recognize similarities both in ideas and in nature, and to the degree that each was able to discern the similarities in observed differences, to *that* degree did significant achievement result.

Unquestionably, the unique points of view expressed on the matter of teaching a child to read have considerable merit when understood in the specific context of using a specific methodology with a specific child in a specific classroom. As yet, however, no universal point of view with regard to the successful teaching of all children has been accepted; possibly none will ever be. The matter of reading method while stable in the theory is precarious in the practice.

At once, then, an advocate of a point of view with regard to the teaching of reading, must admit that the point of view is acceptable only as a part of a total system of language development which must be classified according to:

1. The unique language development of the learner as conditioned by heredity and environment.
2. An understanding of the preferred neurological system utilized in sound-symbol learning.
3. The specific reading materials and teacher methodologies which are or are not compatible with that unique, preferred neurological system.

Under discussion in this fifth Perspectives Volume are nine discrete reading approaches of interest and scholarly investigation. The reading methodologies, materials, and rationale for the various systems of instruction employed within these nine approaches, however, are considerable. Wide differences exist within the language experience area, for example, in terms of degrees of formal structure employed in word skills development. In greater measure, perhaps, do differences exist in basal reader systems and phonetic systems. To suppose that all linguistic systems or all individualized systems were similar would do insult, I am sure, to the proponents of these uniquely developed systems within the wider areas of reading approach.

I would then, at the outset indicate that no incompatibility should exist or need exist among advocates of these nine areas of reading scholarship. Further, it would appear in light of the reading failure which persists in our schools that perhaps certain methodologies and materials, in varying degrees of intensity, from any number of unique systems, among any number of general areas, might very well be necessary to effectively teach one child to learn to read.

This discussion, I know, is beyond the range of my assigned topic, yet I am convinced that major improvements in reading instruction are still to be made, that knowledge of procedures for differentiating instruction in terms of what now appear to be conflicting methods is yet to be appreciated, that the search for adequate neurological diagnosis still lies before us, and that the immense and major task of developing a classification model is the challenge that must be accepted if every child is to learn to read.

Early Letter Emphasis Approaches

It seems that a primary responsibility of this writer would be to define what precisely is meant by early letter emphasis approaches as those approaches would be distinct from phonetic approaches or linguistic approaches.

In theory, phonetic approaches utilize both auditory and visual clues at once, and establish the sound-symbol relationship as the first accomplished relationship essential to reading success. This contrasts with certain early letter emphasis approaches which stress visual discrimination training followed by activities in visual-auditory correspondences.

In this latter regard, the early letter emphasis systems are closer to linguistic systems (9) which are based on pupil knowledge of the alphabet, including the ability to name the letters, which understood scientifically, may be defined as reading.

We might say, then, that phonetic approaches begin by teaching the letters from the sounds and the linguistic approaches begin at the point where the pupil can interpret symbols.

If early letter systems differ in any way from the various phonetic or linguistic systems, it is in the matter of visual and/or auditory emphasis and in the sequence of the skills activities as outlined within the systems.

With either approach, phonetic or linguistic, the "early letter knowledge" advocate would find much in common at our present level of relative ignorance, and much more in common if enough were known of preferred neurological systems employed in auditory-visual learning, and of early diagnosis of perceptual abilities.

The early letter emphasis approach, then, is one which encourages the intensive teaching of the letters early in the reading readiness program.

The approach is basically visual-auditory and usually the visual discrimination of letter skills are taught first.

74093

Once we have defined, or at least attempted to define, the early letter emphasis approach, it is necessary to determine if letter knowledge, as such, is *predictive* of success in first grade reading, or if letter knowledge is *causative* of achievements in early reading skills development.

There is ample research evidence to indicate that letter knowledge is indeed predictive of reading success. Studies by McHugh (*17*), Kingston (*15*), Barrett (*2*), and Durrell (*7*), clearly indicate this positive relationship.

If, in fact, letter knowledge is predictive of success in grade one reading, which particular aspects of letter knowledge contribute most meaningfully to that achievement?

The classic study by Durrell (*7*) identifies several levels of letter knowledge:

1. Ability to directly match letters (upper and lower case).
2. Ability to match letters shown (upper and lower case).
3. ,Ability to identify letters named (upper and lower case).
4. Ability to name the letters (upper and lower case).
5. Ability to relate upper to lower case letters.
6. Ability to write letters.

In an excellent statistical treatment, McHugh (*17*) indicated that the ability to identify letters named and the ability to name the letters correlated most significantly with success in grade one reading.

Regarding the causative relationship between letter knowledge and successful grade one reading achievements, a distinction must immediately be made between:

1. Letter knowledge gained by relatively uncontrolled learning processes.
2. Letter knowledge gained through controlled learning experiences.

Though the distinction might seem trivial to some, to this speaker it is fundamental to an understanding of the importance of early letter emphasis in formal reading-readiness programs.

Both aspects of the distinction above were examined in the original Durrell study.

For 2,188 grade one pupils with a mean IQ of 109, Nicholson (*7*) reported mean scores of 16 (upper case) and 12 (lower case) on the ability to identify letters named.

The letter knowledge achievements of those pupils in the September testing prompt the following questions:

1. What were the characteristics of the kindergarten programs in

those communities in which the research was conducted?

2. Which home backgrounds or parental influences might have affected letter achievements?

The answers to the previous question were, of course, beyond the scope of the original study. If the study could in fact be duplicated, it would be extremely difficult to devise instruments which could objectively describe learning activities in uncontrolled home environments.

In an experimental sub-study Linehan (7) reported the achievements of two groups of grade one pupils with control-variable scores comparable to those of the total population.

A control group (n=300) followed a developmental reading program with incidental letter instruction.

An experimental group (n=312) followed a systematic program of presentation of letter knowledge and phonics development with an incidental program of word recognition development.

Satistically significant differences on measures of oral reading, paragraph meaning, and phonic ability favored the experimental group. Smaller score differences in word classification abilities, silent reading, and word recognition ability likewise favored the letter emphasis group.

On the basis of this study, some tentative assumption might be made that programs stressing early letter mastery are causative of higher February and June first grade reading achievements.

Significant questions bearing on the Linehan (7) results have implications for developing reading readiness programs in the kindergarten year:

1. Would kindergarten readiness programs stressing early mastery of letter names and sounds produce higher September letter achievements?

2. Would superior letter achievements in September of grade one produce higher February and June reading achievements?

Currently, two treatment groups of a three treatment group design are participating in the United States Office of Education Cooperative First Grade Research Project.

Six hundred grade one pupils with a mean IQ of 95, significantly below the mean of the Linehan group, and living in lower middleclass to deprived areas, began grade one with higher mean scores on the Ability to Identify Letters Named test. On this measure, mean scores of 22 upper and 20 lower case letters named were recorded for treatment groups II and III of the USOE Project 2650.

The description of the early letter emphasis approach which produced these relatively high September letter knowledge achievements, follows.

It is difficult for me at this juncture to perceive early letter emphasis programs as differentiated by the kindergarten year or the grade one year. The program herein described is one which starts for many pupils in the kindergarten year and is continued in grade one; while for other pupils the program starts in grade one and continues, hopefully, until success in reading is achieved.

The Skills Program

Seven levels of visual and auditory discrimination ability comprise the letter program for the kindergarten year:

1. Ability to directly match letters.
2. Ability to match letters shown.
3. Ability to identify letters named.
4. Ability to name the letters.
5. Ability to relate upper to lower case letters.
6. Ability to recognize consonant sounds (in the beginning, ending, and medial positions).
7. Ability to recognize blend sounds.

Individual Differences

It was hypothesized from the inception of the program that not all children would be physiologically, neurologically, emotionally, or socially ready for early letter emphasis programs at the same time.

This understanding prompted the search for objective measures of pupil capacities and abilities which would indicate when the formal letter readiness activities should begin.

We are still searching for those objective measures.

In the absence of objective measures, the decision as to when a formal letter emphasis program should begin may be easy or difficult.

The decision as to when to begin is easy when teachers are confident in their teaching procedures, have ample educational materials, are sensitive to pupil failure, and are successful in their initial efforts.

The decision as to when to begin is difficult when teachers are not confident in their methods, do not have adequate materials, and will not accept the fact that pupils must sometimes fail in order to learn.

Obviously, a sensitive, successful teacher is the best objective measure thus far devised to determine when formal educational programs should start. Indeed it is perhaps that *when* to begin is not nearly as important as the confidence of the teacher *in* beginning.

In this, the third year of our research, we find that the teachers started letter activities earlier in the kindergarten year, with increased success in both group instruction and with the assignment of pupil-directed activities.

Intensity of Practice

Regardless of particular method used, an often overlooked factor in beginning reading instruction is the amount and the type of pupil practice necessary to acquire skill mastery.

A significant problem in the early letter emphasis program under discussion was the paucity of commercially prepared materials for implementing the design of the program.

If we were to respect individual differences in classroom practice as well as in developmental theory, the educational materials to differentiate and intensify letter knowledge learning would have to be locally produced.

During 1962, 1963, and 1964, the mothers of pupils enrolled in the kindergartens of the Clovis, California schools met one morning per week during the school year to build the necessary materials and to improve those which had been previously developed and found to be inadequate. At the same time the mothers (and occasionally a father) were specifically instructed on the letter skills which the use of such materials would develop.

It was indeed a wholesome community effort.

Grouping in the Kindergarten

If one accepts the realities of individual differences in learning, grouping for instruction in the kindergarten classroom is essential.

I do not believe that a single advocate of formal and early intensive letter readiness programs would deny the existence of physical and intellectual developmental levels at which success in learning might be assumed. Indeed it is distressing at times to be accused of starting formal instruction too early for some and then to be doubly indicted for grouping pupils in order that instruction be delayed for others.

The kindergarten classrooms in which early letter readiness programs are found are not so markedly different from traditional ones. Clay, blocks, crayola, beads, and manipulative toys are regularly used and enjoyed. Hopefully, where these materials are found and in whose hands they are found, should be determined by the teacher's understanding of the developmental level of the individual pupil under consideration.

Efficient learning experiences of early letter emphasis programs should range from non-symbol activities, including oral language development, to letter experiences associating grapheme and phoneme.

Teacher-Directed Activities in Early Letter Approaches

All teacher-directed activities are designed to be used ultimately in pupil-directed activities. The amount of practice necessary to master skills, following direct teacher instruction, must really be predicated on the amount of self practice the learner can effect.

Sub-grouping in the regular classroom is often ineffective because the materials for practice are often entirely teacher directed or often are not directly related to the sub-skills weakness to be improved.

A first step in the system here described is direct instruction in puzzle completion, an activity by most kindergarten pupils. Puzzles with larger individual pieces and a smaller number of pieces are used in this first step.

Upper case letters are printed on the back of each puzzle piece and on the mat into which the puzzle fits. The pupils are instructed to complete the puzzle by directly matching the letters rather than by forming the picture in the puzzle. Once learned, this puzzle completion game becomes a pupil-directed activity to be experienced as often as necessary to ensure direct mastery of upper then lower case letters.

The puzzles become increasingly more difficult to the point where 48- and 54-piece puzzles are used.

By printing upper case letters on the puzzle pieces and lower case on the puzzle mat, the skill of ability to relate upper to lower case letters is taught and then practiced.

Individual bingo cards with letters imprinted are also used for direct matching practice as well as for the development of higher letter skills. These cards are color keyed and contain new as well as previously learned letters.

Spinners of the type normally found in many children's games are also used and are color keyed to accompany the letter bingo cards.

It is not uncommon to see kindergarten pupils busily engaged in many small group activities stressing letter skills. I am of the opinion that these early experiences in self directing-self correcting activities significantly contribute to later reading success.

The game idea is used in both teacher-directed and pupil-directed activities. Peg boards, individual play cards, parking lots with lettered cars and stalls are used in teaching the visual and auditory discrimination skills.

It is emphasized that not all children participate in these letter-emphasis activities. It has been our experience, however, to discover that most want to participate.

Higher letter skills of learning the names of the letters and learning letter sounds require more teacher direction. The use of pictures stressing beginning sounds and every pupil response letter cards are employed. Each teacher-directed activity lends itself, however, to pupil-directed practice. It is not unusual to observe the teacher using a set of materials for teaching beginning consonant sounds one day and to observe the pupils using the same materials for practice on the next.

Obviously, practice arrangements of this kind require highly developed organizational plans for the filing of materials and thorough pupil understanding of that system.

Formal instruction programs in the early primary years are often criticized on the basis of their structured aspects. If learning is predicated on the learner, however, and if intensive practice will overcome sub-skills weaknesses, and if this intensive practice is largely pupil-directed, then order and organization are essential in establishing a favorable learning environment.

Greater degrees of freedom are always found in those classrooms where the tasks are well defined, the educational materials organized for immediate pupil use and the responsibility placed upon the learner for maintaining both skills progress and discipline.

September Grade One Measures

On entrance to first grade, a series of letter tests ranging from direct matching of letters to knowledge of consonant sounds is administered.

The purpose of these tests is to measure letter knowledge achievements as well as to reveal sub-skills weaknesses in both visual and auditory discrimination areas.

The intensive small group procedures utilized in the kindergarten program are likewise employed in grade one to overcome letter-knowledge deficiencies.

For those pupils scoring 20 and above on the ability to recognize letters named test (upper and lower case), reading instruction in the first pre-primer is started immediately. Letter-knowledge deficiencies are noted and both teacher-directed and pupil-directed letter instruction are conducted in addition to the developmental procedures of the basal reading program.

For pupils scoring below the established norms, primary emphasis is on letter mastery before placement in the basal reading program, though for some pupils the supplementary letter program is conducted currently with the developmental basal program.

Evaluation

The major question to be answered regarding an intensive early letter emphasis program is: Do the achievements of grade one pupils, as measured in June, justify the early intensive teaching of letter names and sounds in developmental reading programs? The answer to that question must await the final evaluations which will be administered in May, 1965.

The results of the control variable testing administered to three Treatment Groups (n=1100) in September in the current Cooperative First Grade Research do, however, shed considerable light on the effectiveness of early letter knowledge programs.

Two of these Treatment Groups participated in a program of intensive letter instruction while one did not.

Two measures used in an analysis of variance were administered in September, 1964.

> —Murphy Durrell Reading Readiness Test
> Sub Tests:
>> Phoneme knowledge
>> Ability to recognize letters named
>> Learning rate
>
> —Metropolitan Reading Readiness Test, Form A
> Sub Tests:
>> Listening   Copying
>> Matching   Alphabet
>> Number knowledge

There were no significant differences in IQ scores among treatment groups. Teacher experience and training, socio-economic factors, and amount of kindergarten participation were the same for all three groups.

For phoneme knowledge, letter knowledge, and learning rate statistically significant differences at the 1 per cent level of confidence favored the two early letter program treatment groups.

On the Metropolitan Readiness sub tests, number, and copying statistically significant differences at the 5 per cent level of confidence favored the treatment groups which followed an early letter emphasis program.

Additional sub tests of word meaning, matching, and alphabet knowledge significantly favored the experimental treatments at the 1 per cent level of confidence. Total Metropolitan Readiness score likewise favored the two letter knowledge groups at the 1 per cent level of confidence. There were no significant differences on the listening sub test.

Subjective evaluation of these results, while suspect among those more "academically" inclined should, I believe merit forum within our own professional fraternity.

In administering these measures, the examiners, all experienced grade one teachers not connected with any of the involved school systems, reported much difficulty in conducting the tests for the control group.

Three observations were regularly reported:

1. Pupils in the control group had considerable difficulty in following directions.
2. It was difficult for pupils in this treatment group to sustain attention during the conduct of the examination.
3. Pupils had difficulty holding their place so that the responses would refer to the specific item being measured.

Additional individual testing was conducted and an analysis of those results will be made in the final report to the United States Office of Education.

I would like to present a tentative hypothesis relative to the relationship between early letter emphasis and successful first grade reading.

I do not believe that letter-knowledge achievement, as such, is causative of superior reading abilities in grade one. I believe, however, that the process by which a pupil learns symbols, of whatever nature, develops two fundamental skills essential for reading success:

1. Attention and persistence in learning.
2. Ability to follow directions.

It is the mastery of these two skills, by whatever program achieved, that ultimately results in beginning reading success.

For the skill of reading, attention and persistence in learning may be perceived as basically physical—the ability to maintain and sustain visual sense attention while accommodating the auditory stimulus to the letter or word.

The latter skill, ability to follow directions, is basically mental and is developed through an instructional program of increasing complexity ranging from oral-object relationships to written directions.

It is my contention that these skills are most efficiently improved through early letter emphasis approaches prior to or concurrent with basal reader approaches.

REFERENCES

1. Balow, Irving H. "Sex Differences in First Grade Reading," *Elementary English,* 40, March 1963.

2. Barrett, Thomas C. "Visual Discrimination Tasks as Predictors of First Grade Reading Achievement," *The Reading Teacher,* Vol. 18, No. 4, January 1965.

3. Birch, Herbert, and Lefford, Arthur. *Intersensory Development in Children,* Monographs of the Society for Research in Child Development, Vol. 28, No. 5, 1963.

4. Bowers, Norman D. "Meaningful Learning and Retention, Task and Method Variables," *Review of Educational Research,* Vol. XXXI, No. 5, December 1961.

5. Brzeinski, Joseph E. "Beginning Reading in Denver," *The Reading Teacher,* Vol. 18, No. 1, October 1964.

6. Davy, Ruth Ann. "Adaptation of Progressive Choice Method for Teaching Reading to Retarded Children," *American Journal of Mental Deficiency,* 67, September 1962.

7. Durrell, Donald D. and others. "Success in First Grade Reading," *Journal of Education,* Boston University, February 1958.

8. Durrell, Donald D., and Murphy, Helen. "Boston University Research in Elementary School Reading, 1933-1963," *Journal of Education,* Boston University, December 1963.

9. Fries, Charles C. *Linguistics and Reading.* New York: Holt, Rinehart and Winston, 1963.

10. Getzels, Jacob, and Elkins, Ruth. "Perceptual and Cognitive Development," *Review of Educational Research,* December 1964.

11. Heldreth, Gertrude. "Linguistic Factors in Early Reading Instruction," *The Reading Teacher,* December 1964.

12. Ilg, Frances. "The Child from Three to Eight, Implications for Reading," *New Dimensions in Reading,* A Report of the Nineteenth Annual Conference and Course on Reading, University of Pittsburgh.

13. Karlson, Bjorn. "Children's Reading and the Linguistic Structure of Language," *The Reading Teacher,* December 1964.

14. Ketchum, E. Gillet. "Neurological and Psychological Trends in Reading Diagnosis," *The Reading Teacher,* May 1964.

15. Kingston, Albert H., Jr. "The Relationship of First Grade Readiness to

Third and Fourth Grade Achievement," *Journal of Educational Research*, October 1962.

16. Lewis, Edward R., and Lewis, Hilda. "An Analysis of Errors in the Formation of Manuscript Letters by First Grade Children," *American Educational Research Journal*, January 1965.

17. McHugh, Walter J. "Indices of Success in First Grade Reading," unpublished independent research, California State College, Hayward, 1964.

18. Muehl, Siegmar. "The Effects of Visual Discrimination Pretraining with Word and Letter Stimuli on Learning to Read a Word List in Kindergarten Children," *Journal of Educational Psychology*, August 1961.

19. Otto, Wayne. "Hierarchical Responses Elicited by Verbal and Pictoral Stimuli," *American Educational Research Journal*, November 1964.

20. Popp, Helen M. "Visual Discrimination of Alphabet Letters," *The Reading Teacher*, January 1964.

21. Sandstedt, Barbara. "Relationship between Memory Span and Intelligence of Severely Retarded Readers," *The Reading Teacher*, January 1964.

22. Suchman, J. Richard, and Aschner, Mary J. "Perceptual and Cognitive Development," *Review of Educational Research*, December 1961.

23. Van Riper, C. "A Speech Pathologist Looks at Reading," *The Reading Teacher*, April 1964.

24. Walters, Richard, and Doan, Helen. "Perceptual and Cognitive Functioning of Retarded Readers," *Journal of Consulting Psychology*, August 1962.

RALPH F. ROBINETT

DADE COUNTY PUBLIC SCHOOLS
MIAMI, FLORIDA

9. A "Linguistic" Approach to Beginning Reading for Bilingual Children

ANY CONSIDERATION of the teaching of beginning reading to children who are called bilingual in the United States might well begin with a discussion of what we mean by *bilingual,* for in our schools we have come to use the term to cover a wide range of linguistic phenomena.

The Term *Bilingual*

A child entering first grade may be called bilingual for the obvious reason that he speaks two languages. His classmate may be called bilingual if he speaks a single language other than English. Our label of bilingual for this child seems to be an expression of intention on our part to equip him to function linguistically in a school situation in which English is the medium of instruction. A third child may be labelled bilingual because his parents were born in a non-English speaking country. Such a child might be, in fact, an English speaking monolingual classified as bilingual because his dialect is non-standard, or he might be so classified because of his surname or his socio-economic status in the community. Unfortunate as it may be, we use the term *bilingual* in a variety of situations not covered by its literal meaning.

Overview of the Dade County Program

The beginning reading program currently being developed in Dade County for bilingual children has been strongly influenced by structural linguistics. Both in the language learning experiences which precede and accompany reading instruction and in the selection and organization of

132

the reading content itself, there has been an effort made to incorporate the newer insights into the nature of language and the nature of its graphic counterpart. At the same time, there has been made an equally important effort to maintain good pedagogical practices of conventional developmental reading programs, using referential content which reflects time-honored traditions of children's literature. This two-year program is embodied in a set of materials called *Miami Linguistic Reader Series,* and has been developed around ten major linguistic and pedagogical premises.

Premise 1: That the referential content of beginning reading materials must deal with those things which time has shown are truly interesting to children.

What do we ask the child to read about? Does the content from the outset provide reading experiences which guide the child to love books and want to read? In the *Miami Series,* an effort has been made to give the beginning reading materials some of the appeal of children's folklore and of children's trade books. Books do not have to be dull just because they are for beginners, nor should writers of textbooks shield their lack of creativity behind the rationalization that the limitations of vocabulary and structure patterns prevent them from writing interesting material.

The persistent themes and situations of children's stories which have been handed down as cultural tradition do not focus on "normal" families in neat, clean, middle-class communities. They are cross-cultural and draw on the reservoir of common human experiences. They have action and suspense. They have surprise and drama. They have imagination and fancy. And children have a right to expect such qualities in even the simplest of materials.

The stories of the *Miami Series* fall into four groups. In the first group, the characters are all animals that behave as human beings. The first characters are Biff and Tiff, two dogs. Biff, the teacher-father figure, has much to learn from son Tiff. The second story is about the problems of an adventurous kitten who overestimates his capabilities and finds himself in trouble. In the third story we meet Nat the Rat, who is not too good and not too bad. The rest of the first nine stories continue in a similar vein, presenting problems to be resolved by the protagonists, and providing a basis for a consideration of social and moral values. The stories of the second group are adaptations of folk tales such as *Jack and the Beanstalk* and *Rumpelstiltskin.* The stories in the third group might be categorized as "realistic," and those of the fourth group, "Americana."

Premise 2: That the materials must reflect the natural language forms of children's speech.

Linguists, educators, and parents have long reacted against the peculiar dialect of preprimers. "Primer-ese" of the Dick-and-Jane variety has honest roots in a sincere desire to help ease the young mind into the wonderful world of the printed page, but it often violates a basic principle known to linguists and reading specialists alike—that print is (or should be) talk written down. If we take seriously the studies of Ruth Strickland at Indiana and Walter Loban of Berkeley, we must admit that, linguistically speaking, Dicks and Janes are few and far between.

Unfortunately, some of the efforts in linguistically oriented materials have not escaped artificiality in language. Following is a typical "story" in the Fries-Wilson-Rudolph first reader which makes us wonder if the Bloomfieldian dialect is any better stylistically than "primer-ese."

Tag the Bag

Dan is at bat.	Dan can tag the bag.
Dan can bat.	Dan sat on the tan bag.
Dan ran.	Dad had to fan Dan.
Tag the bag, Dan.	

It may be argued that all of these sentences are grammatically possible, but the sentences as they combine into a total context do not seem to contribute materially to overcoming "primer-ese."

Some other materials have intentionally stayed close to the traditional fractured English, such as the beginning materials of Smith and Stratemeyer, in which frogs jump and hop for 61 pages. An example is:

> Zip and Pud jump up.
> Zip and Pud jump in.
> Zip gets wet.
> Pud gets wet.

And in the case of the *Miami Series,* it is not always easy to argue that *Sit, Tiff sit* is any more natural than the *Go, Jane, go* of traditional materials. Language certainly can be judged more accurately when we are dealing with the over-all text than when we are dealing with isolated sentences. Any material which is constructed with rigid controls, whether they be controls of configuration or of spelling pattern, is likely to run aground on the sandbar of phoney English. At best it is a matter of degree.

Still, if we are to guide children to the realization that print represents speech, we must make every effort to bring the graphic and spoken sequences closer together.

A native English-speaking pupil approaching material written in "primer-ese" has the advantage of knowing that the language represented is a special dialect, and his exposure to such a dialect may not affect appreciably his day-to-day language habits. The child who is just learning English, however, is less well equipped to withstand the special dialect, and it may interfere with his development of the basic forms of the language and with his sensitivity to natural sequences of sentences. The concern for the language habits of the pupil learning English leads us to the third major premise underlying the *Miami Series*.

Premise 3: That the child must have aural-oral control of the material he is expected to read.

Much of the effort of American linguists since 1925 has been directed toward the synchronic study of language, and fortunately the nature of American English has repeatedly been the subject of such investigations. The result is that we now have at our disposal considerable scientific knowledge about the English language. The application of this knowledge to the teaching of English as a second language was set in motion by Fries and his colleagues and students after World War II, and the impact of this effort is now beginning to reach the public school level in this country. Audio-lingual programs geared to the American scene where the target language is also the medium of instruction are sprouting up all over the Southwest. Although particulars of these programs vary widely with local philosophies regarding elementary curriculum, there is increasing evidence that teachers are aware of linguistics and are beginning to experiment with its findings.

The oral language experiences provided in the *Miami Series* is one such example of English linguistics applied to second language teaching. The *Introductory* (readiness) *Unit* preceding the introduction of formal reading, and the oral language activities surrounding the reading, attempt to provide systematic, meaningful oral practice on the basic features of American English. The linguistic content for oral mastery is structured in its presentation, taking into account contrasts within the English language system and contrasts between English and Spanish. In the ordering of the linguistic content, less concern has been shown for the "logical" sequences and manipulation typical of materials produced under the direction of linguists, and more concern has been shown for the communication aspects of the language experience and the relevance of the language to the content of the pupils' reading material.

Premise 4: That in developing beginning reading materials the focus must be on the skills involved in the process of reading rather than on the uses to which reading is put after the process is mastered.

The uses of reading as they relate to the development of a wide range of skills in thinking and appreciation are often pushed further and further down into the grades until a minimal amount of time is left for the development of the mechanics of reading—without which the learner cannot move into the functional and creative reading experiences expected of him. The question raised here is, "Has the learner been provided with adequate opportunity to master the skills he needs in order to do with reading what is expected of him?"

The problems involved in separating the process of reading from the uses of reading do not pose an either-or situation, but rather one of order and balance. The reading programs available to the teacher of bilingual children are usually the conventional developmental series. As we all know, such series have a "big book" which is designed in part to guide class instruction through the cultural experiences and reading mechanics involved in the first preprimer of the reading series. The time-span occupied by the "big book" is relatively short, and further attention to the cultural background and reading mechanics implicit in the reading program stems from the pupils' books themselves. Unfortunately, as soon as the pupils move into their individual preprimers, many teachers tend to emphasize the referential content to the neglect of the reading process over which the pupil still has questionable control.

In many schools where there are large numbers of pupils learning English as a second language, "formal" reading is delayed as much as a year. The delay is usually explained as time needed to develop linguistic readiness, but it is also widely used to extend the time devoted to the introduction of the process of reading, whether this be using commercial materials or language experience charts.

Many feel, as do we of the Dade County project, that less effort should be spent on getting the child ready to read, and more effort spent on getting reading material ready for the child. Rather than delay the intro-duction of reading, the *Miami Series* attempts to combine the language and reading experiences in such a way that they reinforce each other from the beginning of the school year. Additional attention to the process of reading is provided by extending the "big book" experience for several months. For each of the first three pupils' books, the *Miami Series* provides a "big book" which serves as a basis for developing pupil control over the referential and linguistic content of the pupils' book to follow. The primary, though not sole, focus in the "big book" on language and the reading process leaves ample opportunity during the handling of the pupils' book for the development of other types of skills commonly introduced through reading. Continued emphasis on language and the reading process is encouraged through the use of a fourth "big book" and additional charts corresponding to the remaining books in the *Miami Series*.

Premise 5: That the presentation of sound-symbol correspondences in beginning reading should be in terms of spelling patterns rather than in terms of individual letter-sound correspondences.

One of the major influences stemming from linguists' interests in beginning reading instruction centers on the alphabetic principle, or more specifically, the principle that there is a pedagogically useful degree of predictability in the relationship between significant sound units in the language and the letter units of the writing system. This principle, so stated, is the essence of phonics in most of its varieties. Linguists are usually quick to disassociate themselves from phonics of any variety, however, for many phonics proponents emphasize the relation of individual letters and individual sounds, whereas linguists are more often concerned with sequences of letters, the patterns of letters, as they correlate with sequences of sounds.

This insistence on the part of linguists that the English writing system is based on patterns of letters and patterns of sounds, and that it is not purely alphabetic on the one hand nor hieroglyphic on the other, leads them to the conclusion that perhaps the first problem in reading in American schools is the lack of beginning materials which reflect the basic patterns of the writing system. Several attempts have been and are being made to introduce the alphabetic principle into materials for beginning reading, such as the materials prepared by Bloomfield-Barnhart, Smith-Stratemeyer, Fries-Wilson-Rudolph, Hall, and Glim. We are unaware of any unified, "linguistic approach" to reading, and we might conclude that many more questions have been raised than have been answered. We must keep in mind, however, that much of the linguists' attention has not been directed to an approach to teaching reading, but rather to the selection and organization of materials to be used.

The know-how of teaching little children to read is generally outside the background, experience, and function of linguists. However, it seems to us quite proper that linguists should raise questions without necessarily being the ones to answer them.

The *Miami Series* attempts to implement the alphabetic principle, both as an aid in developing automatic responses to spelling patterns and as a means of systematizing practice on problems of the English sound system. Following is a comparison of this approach to the spelling system and the traditional approach in a basal series.

The control in spelling patterns is obvious. In the same number of pages of pupil text the *Miami Series* presents only three vowel letters in patterns, while the typical basal series presents all five vowel letters in a great diversity of patterns. What is not so obvious to those unaccustomed to dealing with English as a second language is the potential for practice on sound system contrasts. The troublesome vowel phonemes are concentrated in meaningful, interesting situations and may be contrasted with other vowel phonemes used orally in the language activities. Hence problems intrinsic in pairs such as *sit-seat, slip-sleep* and *pick-peak* are not relegated to pure manipulation drills. Likewise, names such as *King Kim* are presented to help the pupil overcome consonant interferences from his own sound system, as are *Kid Kit* and *Tug Duck* and pairs such as *pig-pick, big-pig,* and *sinking-thinking.* As the pupils progress in the material, they develop the ability to react to more complex contrasts such as *hit-hat-hut-hot* which serve both the spelling pattern and sound segment contrasts.

Premise 6: That grammatical structure as well as vocabulary must be controlled.

The linguistic content of reading material for bilingual children should reflect not only natural language forms and sequences as mentioned earlier, it should also be controlled in such a way that the reading itself reinforces the pupils' oral language development. Although the bilingual child's oral language grows at a much more rapid pace than his ability to handle the printed counterpart, much of his oral language is still imperfect and a still larger part is on the level of understanding rather than on the level of active use. The gradual introduction of grammatical forms and arrangements in the reading allows for a systematic and less hurried practice, and provides additional opportunity for the child to perfect his active control

Spelling patterns in the *Miami Series*			Spelling patterns in typical basal series			
112 pages			112 pages			
1 **Biff** T*iff*	K*id*	p*ick* k*ick*	*Dick* *did*	T*im* w*ith*	*is*	1
t*ip* sl*ip* dr*ip*	K*it* s*it* *it* h*it*	d*ig* p*ig* w*ig*	come			2
			Mother			3
K*im* sw*im*	*-ing* k*ing* s*ing*	*is* h*is*	*go*	*no*		4
			b*all*			5
d*ish* f*ish*	r*ing*	m*ilk*	he*lp*	g*et*		6
w*ish*	s*ink* dr*ink*	m*iss*	loo*k*			7
			J*ane*			8
in p*in*	th*ink*	w*ith*	Father	*want*		9
		sp*ill*	(Fath*er*)	(Moth*er*)		10
			Spo*t*	*not*		11
2 P*ap* n*ap*	f*at* N*at* r*at*	C*ab* R*ab* gr*ab*	(Sally)			12
sac*k* bl*ack*	h*at* th*at* c*at*	r*ab*bit	Sally *at*	*and* *that*	*can*	13
and h*and*		c*at*fish	me	we		14
			down			15
			to			16
3 s*un* r*un*	T*ug* b*ug*	h*um* h*unt*	play	aw*ay*		17
			(aw*ay*)			18
h*ut* c*ut*	*up*	m*ud*	P*uff*	r*un*	j*ump*	19
b*ut*	j*ump* b*ump*	d*uck*	find			20
Bu*zz*		cl*ub*	see			21
			here			22
a	*the*		oh I	you	said the	

of basic features of the language system.

In the *Miami Series,* the grammatical forms and arrangements are controlled, just as are the spelling patterns and vocabulary. The two stories of level One emphasize command forms and the present progressive, as in *Sit, Tiff* and *Tiff is sitting.* Level Two continues the progressive and emphasizes patterns of identification, as *Nat is a rat.* Level Three continues the progressive and identification and emphasizes patterns of description, as *Tug Duck is big,* and *Buzz Bug is a big fat bug.* Also emphasized in Level Three are prepositional phrases, as *in his hut* and *in the sun*. Level four introduces the third person singular *s* and negative statements, as in *Tod Fox drops a dish* and *Tod Fox is not mopping, Tod Fox is not with Mom Fox*. Each subsequent level in turn includes new grammatical patterns to which the teacher gives special attention as she presents the material.

Premise 7: That the child must learn to read by structures if he is to master the skills involved in the act of reading.

Closely related to the need for natural structural sequences and grammatical control in beginning materials is the need to develop the habit of reading by structures. That is, the child must be taught to grasp the grammatical units in what he is reading. Reading by structures is closely allied to phrasing, or reading with expression, and is standard procedure with many expert reading teachers. On the other hand, many otherwise expert reading-teachers have little notion of what constitutes a grammatical unit, and regularly fail to help the child grasp the syntactical, morphological or suprasegmental signals and relationships, which are the basis for comprehension of the printed text. At present, reading by structures remains an important area in reading which has been poorly developed in theory and practice by reading specialist and linguist alike.

The *Miami Series* approaches the problem of teaching pupils to read by structures in each part of the instructional "package," which includes the "big books" and charts, the pupils' books, the seatwork provided for the pupils, and the teachers' manual. In the "big books" and charts there are numerous "pyramid" exercises, or rhythm drills, designed to induce a sense of what constitutes the grammatical units. Controlled introduction and practice of grammatical patterns in the pupils' books and seatwork activities provides further opportunity to focus attention on the relationship among the meaning-signalling units of language. And the guided discussion of the referential content of the stories as provided in the teachers' manuals contributes to tying the reading experience to the stresses, pitches, and pauses of normal speech.

Premise 8: That the learning load in linguistically oriented materials must be determined in terms of the special nature of the materials.

Inasmuch as the criteria for selecting words for "linguistically-oriented" beginning reading material are sharply different from those used for traditional basal readers, it seems proper to raise the question of whether or not the learning burden should be measured in different terms. Should we weigh the learning burden in terms of sequences of letters and space as they form patterns, or should we continue to weigh items as discrete forms, as sight words? Are fifteen or twenty words in a preprimer, each presented as an isolated item, really fewer than thirty or forty items which represent one or two patterns and which are presented as such?

Of the "linguistically-oriented" beginning materials, the Smith-Stratemeyer first preprimer of 64 pages with 21 base forms stays within the range of different words of the traditional developmental series. The first 64 pages of Fries-Wilson-Rudolph have over 40 base forms, twice the number of traditional materials. On the other hand, Smith-Stratemeyer present a much wider range of spelling patterns than do Fries-Wilson-Rudolph. There seems to be at least two highly important factors involved in determining the density of new words in beginning material. One is the strong probability that most pupils approach new printed forms as sight words, even though such words may be regularly spelled; the other is the strong probability that regularly spelled forms, especially when grouped by patterns, will be learned much faster than forms in which no system is apparent.

If we look at only the pupils' books in the *Miami Series* we find some 40 different base forms in the first 64 pages. However, if we take into account the "big books" not characteristic of other "linguistically-oriented" materials but which constitute an integral part of this reading program, the density of new items drops to even lower than the norms for traditional basal pre-primers. The number of different base forms in the beginning of the *Miami Series* is kept low because we believe that these forms are being learned as sight words and need abundant practice. On the other hand, the density of new forms increases steadily as the pupil becomes more proficient in English and as the concept of patterning emerges from the reading material.

Premise 9: That writing experiences reinforce listening, speaking and reading.

In the production of the *Miami Series,* we were inclined toward a functional introduction of the alphabet, giving special attention to individual letters and letter combinations as they appear in the reading materials. The writing activities are complementary and do not constitute a complete writing program as such.

In the *Miami Series,* writing occupies its logical position, following listening, speaking, and reading. As in the case of the other language arts, writing may involve varying degrees of production.

The simplest writing activities are tracing, then copying, and then independent production.

In addition to reinforcing the pupils' language development, the writing helps promote left-to-right orientation and strengthens the pupils' grasp of the spelling patterns being read.

Premise 10: That the materials must be so selected and organized that they will enable the learner to achieve success as he progresses through the materials.

As indicated earlier, the basic features of the English language system are systematically introduced in the *Miami Series,* and the graphic representation follows and reinforces the pupils' oral development. The sequence in introducing the writing system is based on vowel-consonant patterns. Consonant letters in initial position are cumulated and given special attention as patterns of representation emerge. The sequence of vowel patterns for the first 14 of a projected 21 titles is as follows:

LEVEL ONE-A	*i*	as in *sit*	LEVEL SEVEN	*ea*	as in *eat*
LEVEL ONE-B	*i*	as in *sit*		*ow*	as in *cow*
LEVEL TWO	*a*	as in *cat*		*alk*	as in *walk*
LEVEL THREE	*u*	as in *but*	LEVEL EIGHT	*ee*	as in *need*
				y	as in *why*
				ere	as in *where*
PLATEAU REVIEW			LEVEL NINE	*a-e*	as in *came*
				ay	as in *day*
				ou	as in *out*
LEVEL FOUR	*o*	as in *not*		*o*	as in *who*
LEVEL FIVE	*e*	as in *get*			
LEVEL SIX	*e*	as in *he*			
	o	as in *no*	PLATEAU REVIEW		
PLATEAU REVIEW			LEVEL TEN	*i-e-*	as in *like*
				igh	as in *light*
				o-e	as in *some*

In addition to the controls over the language and its graphic representation, we have been concerned with a range of matters affecting readability. In the first twelve titles, the total running words increases from 56 per title to 1465 per title, and the average words per page increases from 2.7 to 31.7. The density of new items per page increases from .38 to 1.3.

Level	1-A	1-B	2	3	Plateau	4
Pages in book	24	24	32	32	32	32
Words in book	56	123	352	401	425	515
Words per page	2.7	5.9	12.1	13.8	14.1	17.7
Sentence length	2.7	4.7	4.4	5.9	6.0	6.1
New items	8	16	23	26	—0—	29
New item average per page	.38	.76	.79	.90	.00	1.00
New item density in running words	$1/7.0$	$1/7.7$	$1/15.3$	$1/15.4$	$0/425$	$1/17.7$
Cumulative page total	24	48	80	112	144	176
Cumulative item total	8	24	47	73	73	102
Cumulative running words	56	179	531	932	1357	1872

In the ratio of new to old items, the change is from one new item in 7 running words to one new item in 26 running words. Average sentence length increases much more rapidly than in conventional basal materials, from 2.7 to 9.57 in a cumulative total of 8202 running words, exclusive of the "big books" and charts.

Level	5	6	Plateau	7	8	9
Pages in book	32	32	32	48	48	48
Words in book	719	760	765	1242	1352	1465
Words per page	24.8	26.2	27.1	28.8	31.4	31.7
Sentence length	6.9	7.3	7.4	8.0	9.0	9.57
New items	29	35	6	49	52	57
New item average per page	1.00	1.20	.21	1.1	1.2	1.3
New item density in running words	$1/24.8$	$1/21.7$	$1/127$	$1/26$	$1/26$	$1/25.7$
Cumulative page total	208	240	272	304	336	368
Cumulative item total	131	166	172	221	273	329
Cumulative running words	2591	3351	4116	5358	6737	8202

Repetition Controls

Repetition of the specific forms introduced has been of conscious concern to us in the production of the *Miami Series,* but the development of sight vocabulary as such is only a short term objective. Inasmuch as one of our basic goals is to help the pupil develop the tools he needs to be "on his own in reading," more important as a long range objective is to develop automatic reaction to the spelling pattern of the English writing system. Repetition controls in the *Miami Series,* therefore, are based on the patterns introduced rather than on individual words as sight words. The name *Biff,* for example, appears 43 times in the first nine books. The

	1st big book	Pupil book 1	2nd big book	3rd big book	Plateau 1-3	Totals
Biff	15	7	9	1	11	43
Tiff	35	14	18	2	24	93
						136

vowel-consonant pattern *-iff*, however, appears 136 times and is picked up again later in the series.

In a like manner, the base form *drink* appears 31 times in Level 1-A, and 26 times in Level 1-B. The word also appears in subsequent stories. The repetitions of the vowel-consonant pattern *-ink* increases geometrically, however, as we add the uses of *think* and *sink* in Level 1-B and *wink* in Level 9. The vowel-consonant pattern *-ing* begins with the verb ending itself in Level 1-A, and is repeated in the uses of *king, ring,* and *sing* in Level 2, and *thing* and *bring* in Level 7. The vowel-consonant pattern *-ill* begins with the uses of *spill* in Level 1-B, and is built up by the uses of *hill* and *still* in Level 5, and *will* in Level 6. As new words are introduced in the reading material, they are contrasted with the words already presented in that pattern, along with other words of the same pattern presented in the "big books," charts, and teachers' manuals.

In the area of grammatical structure, we know of no reading program—basal, phonic, or "linguistic"—which provides in the pupils' texts for planned control and repetition of the grammatical forms and arrangements introduced. In all the materials we have been able to examine, the introduction and repetition of grammatical structure appear to be coincidental to the planned introduction of individual words—be they sight words or words used to teach graphemic patterns.

In the pupils' book of the *Miami Series,* the design for handling the grammatical forms and arrangements is more one of planned introduction and cumulative use than of planned repetition. Obviously, as the range of forms and arrangements we introduce is narrower than that of most programs, the proportionate frequency of a given structural item will tend to be higher. But such coincidental repetition in our pupils' books does not guarantee a greater total number of repetitions than would be typical of a conventional reading program. In fact, a conscious effort has been made in the pupils' books of the *Miami Series* to avoid the manipulative repetition characteristic of basal readers. In the *Miami Series,* we have tried to provide planned repetition of grammatical structure, not through abortive use in the pupils' books, but rather through the "big books" and charts, which are designed in part to give conscious attention to the forms and arrangements appearing in the stories the pupils are reading.

Methodology

As we survey the developments in reading at the present time it seems reasonable to project that in the next few years we may have changes which will affect basal programs as profoundly as did the movement toward vocabulary control and repetition. Indeed, we may be in a decade properly identified as the "advent of linguistics in reading." Unfortunately, in the wide-spread dissatisfaction with reading instruction, problems of content and method are often hopelessly confused. To be sure, method cannot profitably be completely divorced from the materials to be used; on the other hand, the cumulated experience of reading teachers and reading specialists seems to validate a wide range of approaches to teaching reading, regardless of the premises on which the materials were constructed. About all we really know about teaching reading is that not all children learn to read at the same time or at the same rate or through the same stimuli. What we do after grasping these basic facts is a matter of faith in the empirical evidence and pseudo-research available to us.

In the development of teachers' manuals for the *Miami Series,* we were not impressed by reports of how an individual child learned to read under unique circumstances and optimum conditions, for we must be concerned with how to approach large numbers of children under "less than normal" circumstances and marginal conditions. In methodology, we have attempted to harmonize our experience in second-language teaching, our understanding of the graphemic system of English, and the multiple-facet approach to teaching of reading characteristic of conventional reading programs. Many of our conclusions are tentative, to say the least. We believe that fundamentally we have followed the "main stream" in methodology. Inasmuch as the "main stream" is wide, we constantly had to make choices in recommending one procedure or another. At the same time we suspect that the routes not taken often might have been equally profitable.

Our antipathy to the words *always, never* and *don't* does not reflect a desire to straddle fences, but rather a strong conviction that there is no one "right" answer to teaching reading. There are many, however, who clamor for lists of *do's* and *dont's,* so for those who insist, we offer a sampling of our prejudices:

Don't make children indifferent or negative toward reading. Little children are willing to put up with a lot of adult "logic," but the fact that learning to read is a serious matter does not mean that it can not or should not be fun.

Don't try to isolate reading from the rest of the children's day-to-day school activities. The need for system and integrity within a given set of materials does not preclude taking advantage of other opportunities to use reading to satisfy a child's need to communicate and share experience.

Don't be a slave to the manual; use it as it was intended—as a source of identification of the problems being presented and of suggestions for dealing with those problems.

Don't expect a child to know what he has never had a chance to learn. There are usually advanced children in a class who can volunteer to attack a new problem, but the rank and file need direct guidance from the teacher.

Don't confuse language problems and reading problems. If we do insure the linguistic and referential background inherent in the reading material before the child attempts to read, we can not be sure of the source of his problems. And the value of guided oral reading is often underestimated because oral reading for language reinforcement is confused with audience reading.

The steps outlined below represent typical page-by-page reading procedure as recommended in the teachers' manuals of the *Miami Series.* Not all of these steps are applicable at a given point in the *Series,* nor do these steps reflect all of the types of activities that might be employed.

General discussion
    for the referential background of what the pupils are going to read
    for the linguistic background of what the pupils are going to read
    for the relation of the new situation to what the pupils have already read
Imitative, then independent, reading of the printed text
    for the natural intonation, stress, pause and rhythm
    for the context of the new reading items
Reading of multiple-word units within the text
    for grasping the structural units
    for contrasting structural units
Reading of words within the text
    for reinforcement of sight vocabulary
    for reinforcement of spelling patterns
Reading of extensions of spelling patterns
    for reinforcement of patterns
    for application to new words
    for contrast between patterns
Referentially motivated re-reading of text
    for synthesis of linguistic content
    for synthesis of referential content

Writing for reinforcement of new reading items

When the pupil approaches portions of the material with no linguistic or graphemic problems, the focus is shifted to silent reading for content and the development of reading-related skills.

Status of the Project

By September 1965 we expect to have all or most of the twenty-one projected pupils' books of the *Miami Series* available to schools involved in the try-out. Also by that date we expect to have teachers' manuals and seatwork booklets distributed through title fifteen of the twenty-one titles. The last of the manuals and seatwork booklets should be distributed by February 1966. The scheduled production of pupils' texts keeps us six to eight months ahead of actual use in the classroom, and the production of teachers' manuals and seatwork booklets keeps us two to three months ahead of projected need.

Experimentation with the *Miami Series* was initiated during the second semester of the 1963-64 school year with one classroom of Spanish-speaking pupils in Miami Beach. During the 1964-65 school year, the try-out was expanded to include approximately 2,500 pupils in seven states and Puerto Rico. The states are California, Arizona, New Mexico, Colorado, Texas, New York, and Florida. About half of the pupils are in the Dade County area. The pupils involved in the experiment are primarily of Spanish speaking background, though a few groups include Indian children representing various languages, and several groups are "culturally disadvantaged" Negro children.

The groups of Negro children are subjects of a doctoral study comparing the *Miami Series* with conventional reading programs combined with phonics. Preliminary research data on the progress of the other children participating in the try-out will stem, for the time being, largely from comparison of conventional testing program results, but will probably be inconclusive, as the testing instruments are generally considered to be invalid for the type of child involved. Evaluation is further complicated by the fact that (1) no other material we are aware of was designed for the children we are concerned with, (2) many of the children involved in this reading program would not normally be involved in any kind of formal reading program in their early school experience, and (3) the human and financial resources available do not permit the undertaking of full scale formal evaluation within the scope of this production project. It is expected, however, that an adequate evaluation design can be developed to provide objective data as the materials are revised and used more extensively.

Staff and Consultants

The members of the production staff are Paul W. Bell, Herminia M. Cantero, June W. Granger, Rosa G. Inclan, Mildred B. Lash, Judy P. Reeder, and Pauline M. Rojas, with Ralph F. Robinett as production director. Mary E. Perdue was a member of the staff for the first year. The original music accompanying the stories was written by Maria L. Munoz, and the principal illustrator is Rose L. Nash, assisted by Gladys G. Rodriguez. The over-all project of which the production of the *Miami Series* forms a part is sponsored by the Dade County Board of Public Instruction and the Ford Foundation. The project director is Dr. Rojas, with Mr. Robinett as assistant director and Mr. Bell as coordinator.

Specialists with whom we have consulted formally or informally to date are Charles Ferguson, Ross MacDonald, David Reed, Nelson Francis, Albert Marckwardt, Alfred Hayes, Ralph Long, Warren C. Cutts, Theodore Clymer, Emmett Betts, and Marion Anderson. Richard O. White, Supervisor of Special Reading Services of Dade County, has joined us as a regular consultant in the production of the teachers' manuals. Our mention of these specialists does not, of course, imply their endorsement of our efforts, but expresses in a small way our gratitude for their questions and suggestions, and their interest in the problems with which we are struggling.

MILLARD H. BLACK

LOS ANGELES CITY SCHOOLS

10. Beginning Reading Programs for the Culturally Disadvantaged

How many of you ever have lived in a mining town, where the companies dominated the total economic and social structure? The tragedy of Appalachia is not alone in the physical need of the people. The depression years of the thirties showed me that there is more than one kind of poverty and that the most tragic, the most enduring, is that of the mind and spirit, a poverty unrecognized by those whose need is greatest.

Almost forty years ago I was a high school pupil in an Oklahoma mining town, where the population of 20,000 had no public park, no swimming pool, no boys' club, no library, no concerts. To our high school came an Australian, an ex-professional soccer player—not as football coach, but as music teacher. To the 150 of us who were in his band and orchestra and glee clubs, he brought glimpses of a life we had never imagined. He led us to see that there were symphonies and oratorios, as well as the nasal hillbilly songs and the rhythmic, emotional church music we had known all of our lives. It was he, rather than the English teacher, who revealed to us the music that lies concealed in the poetry of 17th and 18th century England.

Here was a teacher who came to a town which, while not poor economically, would have—by almost any other criterion—contended successfully for the doubtful title of "The Most Disadvantaged American City."

I am concerned, as I see vast sums of money being channeled into special school programs, that we school people will view deprivation either as an impersonal blight affecting such and such an area, or will consider only the economic and physical attributes of poverty. I would urge that we look into the needs of the spirit of the boys and girls who live in disadvantaged communities. As we are helping these young people

150

to develop skills which can raise their economic potential, let us at the same time raise their cultural horizon.

What to *include* and what to *exclude* are sobering questions when a speaker is initially planning a discussion regarding beginning reading programs for the culturally disadvantaged. The nearer to the deadline, the greater the concern and frustration one experiences. Several alternatives present themselves: to report only those programs one personally has observed; whether to include those which have been described in detail in school district or departmental publications but insufficiently reported in professional journals; or, as a third possibility, to include as well programs which already have been reported, in order to present a balanced picture of the kinds of experimentation which are being conducted. Whether to discuss only innovations or to include reports of the successful use of traditional methods and materials also must be resolved.

This report will concern itself with programs observed in Southern California; with the City Schools Reading Program, developed in Detroit; and with the experimental use of the Fries linguistic materials in the Philadelphia public schools.

Retardation in total language development among culturally disadvantaged children is an assumption common to many of the programs designed to facilitate growth in reading skill in pupils within this group.

A goal common to all the programs is the improvement of other facets of language, as well as reading.

Factors to be considered in reporting programs for a particular category include:

1. The specific application of methods also useful in many other kinds of classrooms.
2. The difficulties inherent in distinguishing among the needs presented by bilingual children—children who are culturally *different* but who may not possess other characteristics of cultural disadvantage—and by those who appropriately are termed "disadvantaged."

This discussion, with one exception, will focus upon the use of instructional materials or techniques initially designed for use with pupils of many differing backgrounds. The emphasis upon particular problems of the disadvantaged will be reported under the heading "rationale" as each program is described.

Six types of beginning reading programs will be discussed. The title of this particular report—and perhaps its greatest emphasis—is at variance with the subject of this fifth Perspectives in Reading volume: First Grade Reading Programs. I obtained permission to deal with the somewhat broader problem of "Initial Reading Instruction for the Culturally Disadvantaged." The reason for this point of view will be discussed in the last two categories. The types of experimental programs with which this report is concerned are:

1. Specially Designed Basal Instructional Materials
2. Adaptations of Commercial Materials
3. Programmed Basal Instructional Material
4. Phonic Emphasis Used to Supplement Instructional Materials
5. The Language-Experience Approach
6. Pre-School Communication Skills Development Programs

A brief discussion of administrative action designed to enhance the teaching of reading to the culturally disadvantaged also will be included.

Specially Designed Basal Instructional Materials

City Schools Reading Improvement Program.[1] Presses are busily turning out materials designated by authors and publishers as being "especially for the culturally disadvantaged." All too frequently, such materials have been written by persons who have no expertise; or are adaptations or rewrites of an earlier project which might or might not have been successful, either educationally or commercially. In some instances, these so-called specialized materials are little more than "color-me-brown" workbooks. These comments are not applicable to the City Schools Reading Program,[2] which will include all the readers and teaching aids deemed essential to an adequate program of reading instruction.

Rationale. The materials were designed to introduce in beginning reading books non-Caucasian figures in other-than-affluent families. They also attempted to provide models of appropriate language structure through which the pupil might develop good usage.

Description of the Program. Whipple summarizes the unique characteristics of the program in this way:

1. The story characters represent races other than Caucasian, permitting pupils from multi-cultural neighborhoods to more readily identify themselves with the story content.
2. The development of correct speech patterns is promoted in "extraordinary ways." The "natural, familiar speech patterns of the culturally disadvantaged children" were introduced gradu-

ally and in accord with good usage. Thus it was hoped that the pupil could be helped toward correct modes of expression.

3. Unusually high interest value was provided, upon the assumption that because culturally disadvantaged children came from homes where reading is not a common recreational pattern, they have had "no pleasurable experiences in reading and lack the desire to learn to read."

4. Shorter, more numerous books (at the preprimer level) were provided in the city schools Series than is customary, so that the pupil may experience "the pleasure of accomplishment at the earliest possible moment, since he comes from a home in which long-term goals are seldom sought."

5. Social objectives, as well as skill objectives, are emphasized.[3]

The first three preprimers have the familiar family orientation, with this notable difference: the family unit which serves as the story-vehicle is Negro while Caucasians are represented by one little boy.

Whipple reports that "words for the basic vocabulary were chosen with great care. They were selected from a reservoir of words which are widely but incorrectly used. Active verbs were employed in relatively great number, for the child can act them out in the process of learning their meaning. . . . They gave preference to words helpful in developing a strong phonetic program."[4] Extraordinary repetition also was provided.

Belief in the basic educational value of the basal reader approach to initial reading instruction with culturally disadvantaged children was emphasized in the appraisal of the program:

Progress in preparing reading materials for young children results, not from taking an entirely new point of departure, but from utilizing and improving procedures which have been found valuable in classrooms.[5]

Current Status. Detailed results of the use of the first three preprimers have been reported. Six first grade classes started with the city schools preprimers and six classes with the preprimers from a widely used basal reader series, designated in this report (as in the Detroit evaluation) as the "Standard Series." After a certain period, each class switched

[1]Gertrude Whipple. Appraisal of the City Schools Reading Program (Detroit Public Schools, Division for Improvement of Instruction, Language Education Department, Nov., 1963).

[2]Cooperatively developed by the Detroit Public Schools and the Follett Publishing Company.

[3]Whipple, *ibid.*, pp. 1-2.

books. Immediately after completing a series, pupils were tested on that series to ascertain their progress. After both series had been taught, their relative interest appeal was determined, as were pupil attitudes toward characters in the two series.

The social ratings of the schools participating in the study were described by the investigator in this way:

> In summary it may be said that the Caucasian classes participating in this study were above average or superior in social and economic conditions. The Mixed classes ranked lower and included one class in which many pupils faced serious personal problems. As for the Negro classes, one Negro class was somewhat better than average in socio-economic conditions, while the other three Negro classes included the largest proportions of culturally disadvantaged pupils in any of the groups.[6]

The chief findings and conclusions of the experimental use of these materials were reported by Whipple to be:

1. *Racially mixed setting.* It was reported by the teachers that "the children made no mention of the fact that the group of playmates appearing in the city schools books is racially mixed. In all classes, Caucasian, Mixed, and Negro, the children manifested a marked preference for the City Schools Series. When asked to indicate the child character they preferred as a schoolmate and playmate, the children gave highest rank to the Negro characters. . . . Nevertheless, every evidence indicated that the choices were not made on the basis of race. . . ."[7]

2. *Verbal competence.* With the total group of pupils, the City Schools Series was significantly more effective than the Standard Series in promoting word recognition. In oral reading, the differences between the averages of the total population for the two series were slight, but with an apparent trend in favor of the City Schools Series.
   With boys, the experimental materials were much more successful than the Standard Series in promoting oral reading skill. The average score attained by the boys on the City Schools materials was exactly the same as that attained by the girls on the Standard Series.
   The most striking increase in oral reading skill through using the experimental material was for the Negro group; its number of perfect scores in the word recognition test was more than twice that on the Standard

[4]*Ibid.,* p. 1.
[5]*Ibid.,* p. 2.
[6]*Ibid.,* p. 2.
[7]*Ibid.,* p. 30.

Series, a difference which was statistically highly significant. A correspondingly lower average number of errors was observed with the use of the City Schools materials.

3. *Desire to read.* High interest in the experimental material was evidenced, both statistically and in observed reactions of all pupils.

   The City Schools Series also was especially popular with boys, and with the culturally disadvantaged group, most of whom were Negroes.

4. *Length of books.* It was reported by teachers that the smaller number of stories in each of the preprimers (as compared with the Standard Series) was an incentive toward growth in reading, in that pupils appeared to equate success with the early completion of a book.

5. *Social relationships.* While objective comparisons were not possible, the investigators believe that greater social growth occurred with the City Schools materials than with the Standard Series.[8]

This conclusion was reached by Whipple:

> . . . data presented in this report have shown clearly that this city-oriented series is used successfully by culturally-varied urban children including those living in high as well as low socio-economic areas. It meets the needs of urban children in general, and is recommended for unsegregated use because the series as a whole is truly representative of city life.[9]

Research in Progress. Research necessary to the development of the readers is an on-going activity. However, an extensive experiment similar to that which validated the assumptions and content of the first three (of five) preprimers necessarily must be delayed until additional readers have been completed.

Miami Linguistic Series.[10] The Miami Linguistic Series is being used experimentally in a number of elementary schools, both in the Los Angeles City School District and in other districts in Southern California, as a part of a nationwide Ford Foundation Project directed by Pauline M. Rojas. These schools are situated in areas predominantly populated by persons of Mexican-American background. Since Ralph Robinett, Production Director of the Series and Assistant Director of the project, has reported in Chapter Nine on this particular project, it will not be described in this report.

Fries Linguistic Materials. Individuals interested in research on the teaching of beginning reading to culturally disadvantaged pupils through linguistically oriented materials are referred to Chapter Four by Charles

[8]*Ibid.,* pp. 30-32.
[9]*Ibid.,* p. 32.

C. Fries. In an address to the National Council of Teachers of English, Rosemary Green Wilson of the School District of Philadelphia described the initiation of an experiment in the use of linguistic materials.

Current Status. Gains of children involved in this program were described in this way:

1. Great gains in achievement for groups of our least mature, most underprivileged children in mastery of the alphabet, security in reading, enjoyment of reading, retention over the summer. (No nonreaders by end of year.)
2. Great gains from the rapid learners in permitting them at the end of one year to advance into the stage of "productive reading."
3. Concomitant gains in spelling and creative sentence and story writing.
4. Noticeable increase in interest in reading on the part of the boys in our classes.
5. Very favorable reaction on the part of teachers in the experimental program, even those who had taught thirty or more years.
6. Much more meaningful "independent learning activities" could be planned from the earliest stages.

Research in Progress. Continued research in the use of the Fries' materials for beginning reading instruction has been assured through a grant from the U.S. Office of Education.

Adaptations of Commercial Materials

An experiment cooperatively conducted by the Los Angeles City Schools and Occidental College involves the use of commercially produced non-basal reading materials[11] among classes representing different socio-economic groups.

Rationale. The assumptions upon which this research was initiated in the school year 1962-63 included these:

1. Boys would learn to read more quickly if they were instructed in sex-segregated groups.
2. Boys would learn to read more quickly from high-interest material than from traditional primary level materials.

Description of the Program. Approximately 600 children in the first grade in various elementary schools in Los Angeles were taught reading

---

[10]Ralph F. Robinett. Production Director, *Miami Linguistic Readers, Level Four,* Miami, Florida: Board of Public Instruction, 1964, pp. i-ii.

[11]Selma Wasserman and Jack Wasserman. *Sailor Jack and Homer Potts, 1961; Sailor Jack and Eddy, 1961;* and *Sailor Jack, 1960.* Chicago: Benefic Press.

in sex-segregated groups. Other variables, such as the sex of the teacher, the time of day of instruction, and the socio-economic level of the learner, were investigated.

During the year 1963-64, the second year of the research, experimentation was focused upon materials of instruction which were built around the male-interest-oriented books. In 1964-65, a variety of teacher-made supplementary materials, designed to intensify and reinforce the stimulus of the printed symbol, was added to the design. Included were:

1. An introductory sound film, produced by students of Jo M. Stanchfield, Associate Professor of Education, Occidental Colege, and principal investigator in this project.
2. Phoneme boxes, which consisted of teacher-prepared boxes for each child containing pictures which were representative of the letter or group of letters appearing on the card.
3. Individual flannel boards, with appropriate materials and individual blackboards and pocket charts.
4. Paper-bag puppets.

All of the above items were used in the structured readiness program, which emphasizes discovery and recognition of letter-sound relationships, rather than the spending of weeks upon weeks in a readiness activity book.

A wide range of supplementary materials to be used once the readers themselves were introduced also was developed. This included:

1. Printed practice or follow-up activities providing practice in the skill developed in each lesson in the reader.
2. Transcriptions (tapes) to be used at listening centers, providing each child an opportunity to re-read the textbook as he completed follow-up exercises in listening and following directions.
3. Colored slides of the pictures in the texts were used to develop new stories with repetition of the words learned in stories in the readers.
4. Study prints, based on characters and incidents in the books, enabled the teacher to develop the vocabulary of the readers in an auditory situation and provided incentives for pupils to write their own stories.
5. Short stories using the basic vocabulary in new situations were duplicated, providing opportunity for pupils to illustrate these newly learned words.

Current Status. At the end of the year 1962-63 test data revealed that separating the boys from the girls did not help the boys to learn to read better; the girls achieved significantly more in both the experimental and control groups.

Data for 1963-64 again showed no statistically significant differences between the scores of the experimental and control groups, although a trend toward greater growth by the experimental group was observed.

Test data were supplemented by two-hour interviews of each teacher in the experiment.

Stanchfield reached these conclusions concerning the culturally disadvantaged portion of the population of the study:

1. The *activity level* of boys, and particularly those who might be termed "disadvantaged," was much greater than girls.

2. When evaluating *verbal facility,* the teachers reported the frequent use of incomplete and fragmentary sentences, especially among the culturally disadvantaged. Stanchfield observed that when mixed classes were taught, some of the teachers erroneously believed that the boys and girls were participating equally.

3. *Auditory discrimination* was developed with greater difficulty among boys than girls, and that still greater difficulty and differences were observed among those pupils in low socio-economic schools. It was reported that it many times would take boys ten lessons to learn and recognize sounds that the girls could identify in three lessons.

4. *Listening skills* were less easily developed among boys than girls, and among culturally disadvantaged pupils than among those in higher socio-economic levels. It was observed that boys listened more effectively when more than one sense was employed; i.e., they were engaged in parallel use of vision, touch, etc.

5. The maximum *attention span* of first grade, culturally disadvantaged boys tended to be about 12 minutes, while that of girls was almost double that period. However, this observation was qualified by a number of teachers who observed: "It depends upon the activity. Boys can pay attention for a long time if they're doing something active and dynamic, either mental or physical."

6. In the area of *goals and motivations,* teachers reported that culturally disadvantaged boys were less anxious to please the teacher, less self-motivated in learning to read, evidenced less adequate work habits, and were less desirous of assuming responsibility than were boys of average or above-average economic level. Boys as a group also tended to be more deficient in these areas than

did the girls.

7. In analyzing the *interests* of children in the experiment, Stanchfield concluded that culturally disadvantaged pupils did not adequately respond to the situations depicted in currently available
primary reading material.

Research in Progress. Data from the most recent testing of pupils using
for the first time all of the reinforcers developed during the summer of
1964 and included in the description of the program (above) now are
being processed. Analysis of these data will not be completed for some time.

Stanchfield recently received a Rosenburg Foundation grant to pursue
this experimentation in teaching beginning reading from high-interest
materials. Tentative data will be available in 1965-66, but this phase of
her work will not be completed until the end of the school year 1967-68.

Prognosis. If one may generalize from the experiments conducted by
Whipple and Stanchfield which were alike in some respects, it may be
tentatively concluded that beginning reading instruction with culturally
disadvantaged pupils may be more effectively accomplished with materials
which:

1. Provide opportunity, through illustrations and text, for pupils to
   identify themselves with the characters in the stories.
2. Employ speech patterns with which pupils are familiar.
3. Are high in interest value, an item of particular importance when
   teaching boys to read.
4. Provide *many* meaningful repetitions of vocabulary in an interesting manner.
5. Make provision for the shorter attention span evidenced by
   culturally disadvantaged children.
6. Facilitate early and continued success in reading.

Programmed Basal Instructional Material

Sullivan Associates Programmed Reading. The results of instruction
with programmed reading material are being investigated in a cooperative
project between UCLA and the Santa Monica and the Monrovia Unified
School Districts. A Ford Foundation grant has been received by Arthur
Lundaine, Professor of Education; and John McNeill, Associate Professor
of Education, and Harriett Foster, Associate Research Psychologist, are
responsible for the details of the project.

Rationale of the Program. The investigators believe that the Sullivan materials may possess two chief values:

1. Because the pupils may proceed at their own pace, unlimited opportunity to react to each learning task is provided.
2. Because verification of success is inherent in the completion of the learning tasks, continuing gratification or reassurance is provided.

Description of the Program. The Sullivan materials consist of fourteen basic books, seven of which the average first-grade pupil would be expected to complete during the first year of instruction. These are in the familiar workbook-type format and usable only by one pupil; a crayon whose marks disappear after about twenty minutes may serve to reduce the per-pupil cost of the program.

Two kinds of supplementary materials are available: a series of exercises designed to reinforce the skills developed in each book, and storybooks to be read independently in connection with each of the basic instruction books.

Current Status. The project was designed to investigate:

1. The influence of four variables as first-grade pupils were taught to read from the Sullivan *Programmed Reading* materials: (a) intelligence, as evaluated by the Binet or WISC; (2) sex; (3) bi-lingualism; and (4) socio-economic background.
2. Possible interaction effects with program and non-program subjects.
3. The manner in which the program is used by different teachers in the experiment.
4. The effects of using the publishers supplementary materials.

The investigators plan to compare pupils in relation to data obtained on each pupil in September (1964) before instruction was initiated; additional tests are scheduled to be administered in February, May, and October (1965).

In at least two schools, comparisons will be made of pupils of the experimental teachers under program (this year's first grade) and non-program (last year's first grade, now enrolled in the second grade) instruction.

Records of the number and titles of library-type books read by pupils also will be maintained.

No statistically significant differences in the achievement of the control and experimental groups were reflected in the data obtained from the tests administered in February. McNeill and Foster believe that while no conclusions can be drawn at this state of the experiment, that differences in average performance or in variability of individual performance may be found as additional data become available.

Prognosis. At this time, the investigators believe that more rigid controls need to be exercised in the way the programmed materials, as well as other materials of instruction, are used in the classrooms. It is their belief that variables are operative for which controls have not been provided, and that to the extent to which these variables are present the results of the experiment may not be definitive.

Therefore, it is planned that the present project will be completed as scheduled (October, 1965) and that a second phase will be initiated, in which the use of all instructional materials will be subject to less variation.

Phonic Emphases Used to Supplement Instructional Materials

Eclectic Phonetic Emphasis. This title may be a misnomer, for certainly the program observed at Ninety-third Street Elementary School in Los Angeles consists of much more than supplementary phonics drill.

Rationale. The very great concern of the principal of this school, located in a low socio-economic area and comprised almost wholly of Negro pupils, for the development of reading skills was expressed by him in this way: "If a child can read he can do anything; if he *can't* he can do nothing." Consistent with this philosophy, the school program centers around reading, emphasizing to a marked degree this phase of the communication skills.

Description of the Program Materials. In addition to using one of the two state-adopted basal series, workbook-type follow-up materials are used at all reader levels. Teachers also prepare, in addition to the exercises directly extending the skills taught in a particular lesson, oral reading exercises which provide both (1) opportunity to use new vocabulary and (2) exercises in following written instructions. Extensive use is made of cards with which pupils may match upper and lower case letters with a picture which represents the sound of that letter.

While this large school (1500 population) is organized in the customary grade-level pattern, each grade-level is further sub-divided according to reading ability; teacher judgment and the level of the material from which the pupil is receiving instruction are the criteria for this grouping.

At the beginning of the year, all children new to the school, excluding kindergarten and beginning first-grade pupils, are assigned to one of three orientation rooms. Here reading ability is evaluated and permanent assignment is made, usually a period of about one week.

Children who enter the school at other times are similarly tested and assigned by one of two special reading teachers. This is an on-going activity for the school will experience about 100 per cent turnover, with 40 to 50 per cent remaining for three to five years.

A final organizational factor is the use of the "divided day" schedule, approximately one-half the class arriving one hour after their classmates and similarly remaining in school one hour later. The teacher thus has a total group of only 15 or 16, dividing these into the familiar two groups for instruction. In most classrooms, the slow-readers are the ones who arrive at the earlier hour.

When all pupils have arrived in the classroom, the supplementary phonics lesson is held. All children participate, regardless of the reading group to which they belong. This supplementary phonics instruction is initiated at the beginning of the first grade at, according to principal Newell Bowman, "a rate comfortable for the pupils."

At the beginning of grade two, instruction is begun anew with the simplest phonics drills. The purpose of this complete re-teaching is to provide (1) review and (2) initial teaching for pupils who had not attended that school in the first grade.

Reading instruction is initiated in the second semester of the kindergarten as the pupils show readiness. In a kindergarten where there are few high achievers and the formation of reading groups is impractical, those few will be sent to a B1 room for reading instruction. A similar procedure is followed with the occasional child who enters kindergarten and already can read. The principal reports that "from 50 to 70 per cent of the more able kindergarten pupils will be reading by the end of the year, some completing the primer." At least a ten minute daily "story-time" is observed in all classrooms.

Current Status. As would be expected in a school where homogeneous grouping was employed, some classes are reading well above grade level; similarly, some are well below. However, when the scores of all B2 classes were grouped, the achievement appeared to be much higher than would be expected in a school located in a low socio-economic area.

Further evaluation will be made through comparing the achievement of pupils in this school with pupils enrolled in neighboring schools. These comparisons will be made on the data obtained in the regular city-wide testing program.

The Language-Experience Approach

Yet to be discussed are programs which appear to me to offer maximum opportunity for developing the ability of the culturally disadvantaged child to communicate with others through reading. A significant body of research into the abilities of culturally disadvantaged children to communicate establishes this: these children do not listen as well as do more advantaged children; they do not speak as well; they do not read as well; nor do they write as well.

We accept the premise that pupils who have adequate command of oral language learn to read more efficiently and more economically than do pupils who are deficient in listening and speaking skills. This appears to me to point us to two major conclusions as we plan reading instruction for culturally disadvantaged children: (1) the values which accrue from using the language-experience approach; and (2) the importance—the *necessity*—of planned language instruction long before these children are ready to enroll in kindergarten or in the first grade.

The Language-Experience Program at Malabar Street Elementary School. In an address at the Washington Conference on Culturally Disadvantaged Youth, sponsored by the U.S. Office of Education, in May-June, 1962, Rosemary Green Wilson made the following statement:

> The sooner we discard the term "reading program" and begin to think of a "language program," the closer we will be getting to the realities of the situation and a possible solution.
>
> The sooner, also, that we accept the idea that speaking, reading, and writing *cannot* be taught effectively in the same way to children of highly literate parents and to children of completely illiterate or semi-literate parents, the sooner we will reach the public schools' goal of literacy for this and succeeding generations. Thus, will the myth of the same basic reading materials for all children be exploded. . . .

In the Malabar Street Elementary School in Los Angeles a broad experimental program in the total language arts program is being undertaken. Three areas of growth are being evaluated:

1. The language development of pre-school children in a rich, permissive school environment.
2. The language growth of kindergarten children in a similar environment.
3. The growth in reading through the language-experience approach.

Rationale. Among the assumptions upon which this program is based are these:

1. Language growth of children occurs to a greater degree in an environment which stimulates them to think, to explore, and to want to express themselves.
2. Children learn more from a curriculum which is based on their own culture and their own experiences.
3. The skills of listening, speaking, reading, and writing are inextricably interwoven and are most effectively developed through their inter-related use.
4. Among bilingual pupils, the school must capitalize upon the total language ability the child brings with him. The function of the program is expression, regardless of the language used by the pupil. Refinement of expression and skill in the use of English are later goals.

Description of Program. Understanding the child, appreciating his cultural background, and knowing about his home conditions are believed by Mrs. Jacqueline Ayers Hartwick, principal of the school, to be basic to successful working relationships among teachers, pupil, and parents. Teachers are encouraged to visit the homes of pupils; similarly, parents are encouraged in many ways to visit the school, to identify themselves with it, and to understand that the school and home have a common goal for the pupil—his growth in every aspect of his life.

The pre-school program is a cooperative one between the school and California State College at Los Angeles. Pupils in the experimental classroom are free to choose the activities in which they will participate, little control being exercised. However, pupils are stimulated to explore the many interest centers provided in the room. These science, music, art and other activity areas are frequently changed, providing the pupil with many new and, hopefully, interesting things to talk about. The usual large toys, sandbox, etc., are available for their use. Growth in vocabulary and language patterns are being observed closely. The language output of each pupil is recorded at intervals; ways in which new words appear to be learned or to be assimilated into the vocabulary of these three- and four-year-olds are studied. Recently, one boy was present at the storage box when the teacher discovered that a shovel he wished to use in the sand box had been stolen over the weekend. The child said nothing at the time, but some thirty minutes later he began repeating almost interminably "stolen, stolen, stolen. . . ." He then began to practice using the word in sentences, as "My shovel is stolen," "My dog is stolen," using the word in many, many different ways.

In the kindergarten, language activities are encouraged throughout the class period. Much discussion about activities which occurred outside school is encouraged. Stories are read and dramatized. Songs are sung. Art activities are related to things which have been discussed. Purposeful activity from which conclusions or generalizations may be drawn typify the program.

The first-grade reading program in this school, situated in an area populated almost exclusively by Mexican-Americans, emphasizes the use and development of all of the language skills. The program also is characterized by freedom for teachers to use approaches and techniques with which they are familiar and in which they are comfortable. All reading instruction centers around the oral language of the pupils; these children read materials which are meaningful because they have talked about an experience and, after talking about it, have either dictated a story to the teacher—as individual or group experience stories—or have actually done the writing. This kind of instruction is not unique; it occurs in thousands of classrooms each day all over the United States; but I believe that its importance in this discussion of beginning reading programs for the culturally disadvantaged lies in the attempt by the administrator of the school and the classroom teachers to understand the culture of the pupils —both the Mexican heritage which they possess and the events, big and little, which comprise the lives of the pupils and their parents. It is an attempt to develop a meaningful reading curriculum from the daily experiences of the pupils themselves, providing them with an opportunity to develop their listening, speaking, reading, and writing vocabularies out of things and activities with which they have immediate contact.

Efforts are made to employ experiences and activities out of the lives of the pupils themselves as topics of the experience stories. Unusual attention is paid to the use of definitive language by the pupil, help being given him in the selection of an appropriate word and in correct usage.

Through this joint pupil-teacher effort in oral vocabulary and usage, I believe that language control will be more readily developed than through our traditional approaches.

Using the divided-day program, reading is taught at a given time only to one-half the total number of pupils enrolled in the class.

The two major problems in using the experience approach in teaching disadvantaged pupils appear to be essentially administrative in nature:

1. How can the sequential development of word recognition skills be assured without the internal structure provided through the basal reader?

2. How can teachers be helped to become both comfortable and efficient in the use of a non-basal reader approach to instruction? This problem probably is of greater concern with older teachers and with teachers who are below average in performance.

Current Status. The research which supports this program is necessarily divided into two parts: (1) that of the language growth of the pre-school child, which will be reported through a dissertation; and (2) the growth in total language power of pupils in the regular K-6 program of this school. The values which derive from the instructional procedures being employed will become apparent as these pupils move into higher grades and become involved in the regular testing program of the school system, making possible comparisons with the achievement of other schools in the same community and with achievement of earlier pupils within the same school.

Compton Community Demonstration Area. Among the educational programs being sponsored in Los Angeles County by the Economic and Youth Opportunity Agency is one involving selected classrooms in the Compton City, Enterprise City, and Willowbrook Elementary School Districts. The teachers of these experimental classes continue basically to be responsible to the principal of the school in which they work and subject to policies adopted by their respective Boards of Education. They cooperate with the Project Director[12] and Educational Consultant,[13] who are responsible for program planning, supervision and in-service training, and administration of the experimental project. An important administrative aspect of this program is the payment of a salary differential of $80.00 per month; the teacher is thus reimbursed, at least in part, for the extra time and effort involved in the preparation of demonstration lessons, the keeping of research records, continuing attendance at in-service training classes, and in holding parent conferences.

The Enterprise District Project. Experimental programs in this almost totally Negro community include: (1) teaching reading to pupils in grade one and (2) the stimulation and further development of communication skills among pupils now in grade three. This latter program, emphatically

---

[12]Don Hodes, Project Director, Economic and Youth Opportunities Agency, Enterprise City School District, Compton.

[13]Thelma Henney, Educational Consultant, Economic and Youth Opportunity Board, Los Angeles.

not a remedial reading program, later may be extended to grades two and four.

Rationale. The first grade program, recognizing the language and experiential deficit found among disadvantaged children, attempts to:

1. Identify pupils at the end of the kindergarten program who are potential failures in reading.
2. Provide first-hand experiences which will stimulate pupils toward increased self-expression.
3. Provide, where possible, concrete materials for developing abstractions in all phases of the curriculum.
4. Assures success in initial reading experiences.
5. Stimulate general language growth.

Description of Program. Because of the essential similarity in goals and procedures among the various first grade classrooms in the total Demonstration Area project, the reading program at the McKinley school has been selected as being representative of the entire group.

The 25 pupils in the room were cooperatively selected by the kindergarten and first grade teachers, with the assistance of the principal and school psychologist, during the last weeks of the school year. The major criterion was the language immaturity displayed by these kindergarten pupils in comparison with their peers. A deliberate effort was made, according to Mr. Hodes, to select the pupils least likely to learn to read during their ensuing first grade experience. Five reading groups were formed very early in the fall, the teacher working with each group from 10 to 20 minutes. The basic reading lesson generally consists of a group dictated experience story. Reading and continued use of this story follow the familiar pattern. After the discussion and dictation have been completed, pupils individually illustrate some phase of the story; the teacher moves from child to child, writing for each a story to accompany his own drawing. These personal stories are bound in individual books, and repeatedly re-read.

Most instructions to the class as well as to individuals are printed and given orally only when needed; pupils read the instructions aloud before complying. Such statements as these are used:

Come to this chair.

Get ready to go out to play.

The language-experience approach is supplemented by twice-weekly use of preprimers, a related activity book, and a multitude of tradebooks.

Concerted and continued effort is made to have the pupils speak in complete sentences, a task requiring much questioning and repeating by both teacher and pupils.

Many school and neighborhood walks are taken. The class has been on "Listening Walks," "Leaf Walks," and "Smell Walks," among others. The group returned to check on things which had been observed and reported.

A unit in the social studies program, an adjunct in this classroom to language arts development, concerned—at this early age—professional and vocational choice. Under the topic "I Want To Be," pupils had described their ambitions and recorded the kinds of training required.

Parent cooperation is consistently developed. They were invited to the school to discuss the program in its inception, both by the principal and the president of the PTA. Of the 25 sets of parents, 16 came.

Current Status. The chief problems are reported to be parent pressures engendered by the informal nature of the program and local district policies making retention mandatory when certain norms are not achieved.

Research in Progress. While comparison with control groups is not anticipated, growth will be evaluated with the Calfiornia Test of Mental Maturity and with the Lee-Clark reading readiness test. It is expected that individual anecdotal records will provide the greatest help both in assessing the growth of pupils and in recommending curricular or administrative change.

Youth and Economic Opportunity Board—Los Angeles City Schools Pre-School Education Program. The final project to be discussed is one directed toward early intervention in the pattern of language development of the culturally disadvantaged child. Pre-school classes were established in November, 1964, in two neighboring schools in a low-income community populated almost entirely by Negroes.

Rationale. The basic assumptions of the program are that children who live in culturally or economically disadvantaged areas:

1. Are deficient in experiences which prepare them for success in school.
2. Lack motivation toward achievement in our contemporary school programs.
3. Are deficient both in language background and in the total spectrum of communication skills.
4. May, through educational intervention, be re-oriented in their attitudes toward school and may be helped to develop skills necessary to this success.

Description of Program. The project was designed for pupils who were, upon enrollment, between 3.9 and 4.4 years of age. Two experimental classrooms were established; one of the programs was designed to provide maximum teacher-pupil guided interaction, with the pupils being directed in their movement to and from and in their participation in, activities relevant to the rationale described above. The second program envisioned equally detailed planning by the teacher, but much greater pupil-choice or selection of activities in which he would participate. In this report, the first program will be referred to as Program One; the second, as Program Two.

Goals of the programs are basically similar. They have been defined as the development of:

Physical Growth

Intellectual Growth

Social-Emotional Growth[14][15]

The curriculum of the two projects also is basically similar. It has been defined for Program Two as developing:

   I. Sensory Perception

  II. Oral Language Understanding and Usage

     A. Listening for Directions; to answer questions; to enjoy stories and poems; to learn the names of things; to comment on a topic; etc.

     B. Speaking his name; telling his age; discussing and conversing; helping to plan activities

     C. Learning finger plays; nursery rhymes, stories, and poems

 III. Music and Rhythms

 IV. Social Studies Awareness and Understandings

     A. Becoming aware of the geography of the home, school, and community

     B. Learning about time, as it related to work, play, and rest

     C. Developing a feeling of civic responsibility, through caring for pets; helping to care for the room and equipment; and learning about the flag and about various holidays

  V. Pre-Reading Understandings

---

[14]Bernice Christenson, "Pre-School Project 1964-65: 102nd Street School," Los Angeles City Schools, Division of Instructional Services, Curriculum Branch (Experimental Publication), January 1965.

[15]Los Angeles City Schools, Division of Elementary Education, "Experimental Pre-School Projects, 1964-65."

      A. Auditory Discrimination

      B. Visual Perception

      C. Language Usage

  VI. Arithmetical Understandings

 VII. Science Awareness

VIII. Art Experiences

  IX. Enrichment Activities, including trips to the: zoo; park; market; pet store; library; department store; shopping center; the beach; through the neighborhood; to the park on picnics

   X. Outdoor Activities and Equipment, including: wheel toys; jungle gym; balls; sandbox; playhouse; water table; paint easels

  XI. Health and Personal Cleanliness

      A. Developing an understanding of function of parts of the body

      B. Developing habits of personal hygiene

      C. Developing habits of good grooming

 XII. Parent Program

      A. Home activities

      B. Community activities

XIII. Body and Self

      A. Awareness of body and its parts

      B. Eye-hand coordination[16]

As was stated earlier, elements of the two instructional programs appear to be similar. Marked differences in the implementation of the programs were observed, in accordance with the design of the experiment. In Program One, the children are divided into three clusters, with an adult guiding and working with the children. While pupils generally are expected to rotate among their activities with the cluster of which they were members, individual selection of activities is possible within the cluster; greatest freedom of choice obtains in outdoor activities. The membership of the clusters varies from time to time, permitting the most able to progress at optimum rate. In Program Two a number of different interest centers have been established, with pupils generally being free to choose the center or activity in which they wish to participate. Providing an opportunity for the pupil to communicate with both adults and peers on an individual basis is one of the goals of the program.

The programs differ in terms of personnel, both salaried and volunteer.

---

[16]Bernice Christenson, "Proposed Outline for Pre-School Education for Low Socio-Economic Level," Los Angeles City Schools, Division of Instructional Services, Curriculum Branch, November 1964.

Program One employs a full-time teacher, 1 1/5 paid assistants, and the daily help of the mothers of two children in the class; these parents serve on a rotating basis. Parents are reported to have been very responsible in their attendance, and enthusiastic and cooperative in the assistance they have given. This opportunity for direct training of the parents is one of the strengths of the program.

An additional strength of Program One is a one-hour weekly group conference among parents and teacher. Here the teacher attempts to extending the understanding of the parents of the developmental patterns of the four-year-old child in addition to interpreting to them the curriculum. This has provided a base for continuing understanding between the school and home, and the larger community.

Program Two employs one teacher, one paid helper, and one volunteer assistant from a women's organization.

All personnel involved in the programs, as well as the principals of both schools, have commented on the regularity of attendance of the pupils, the unusually low transiency, and the growth in language experienced by these pre-school children.

Current Status and Research. Newton Metfessel and J. T. Foster[17] have developed "A Comprehensive Curricular and Evaluative Model for Preschool Programs Designed for Educationally (Culturally) Disadvantaged Preschool Children." Metfessel and Foster will compare the growth of children in this program in terms of these criteria:

1. Concept Formation
2. Creativity
3. Instructional Objectives
4. Parental Attitudes
5. Socio-Economic Status
6. Teacher and Teacher Aide Attitudes
7. The Achievement Motive
8. Curriculum Methods
9. Intellectual Abilities

No data are at this time available.

This paper began with a statement of concern that we may focus our consideration on programs *per se* rather than on their effect on the lives of children. In closing I would urge, through these lines from James

---

[17]Center for the Study of Educationally (Culturally) Disadvantaged Youth, University of Southern California.

Baldwin, that we continuingly ask ourselves whether our activities improve the status of a child, whether they enable some disadvantaged pupil to see new horizons of achievement and of hope. Baldwin writes that at the age of fourteen he:

> . . . began to feel in the boys a curious, wary, bewildered despair, as though they were now setting in for the long, hard winter of life . . . it was clear (that they) would rise no higher than their fathers. School began to reveal itself, therefore, as a child's game that one could not win, and boys dropped out of school and went to work.[18]

The concern of every person who has responsibility for education of the disadvantaged is to make of school a place where boys and girls are helped to realize that there is a life other than that they have now, and to help them develop the attitudes and the skills which will enable them to rise "higher than their fathers."

[18]James Baldwin. *The Fire Next Time*. New York: The Dial Press (1963), p. 32.

GUY L. BOND

UNIVERSITY OF MINNESOTA

11. Standards for Evaluating First Grade Programs

A FIRST GRADE READING PROGRAM should be evaluated in terms of its effectiveness in fostering growth in each of the broad objectives of the total reading program. Reading instruction should also be evaluated in respect to the extent that it makes possible the maximum rate of growth of each individual and the extent to which it prevents serious reading problems from developing.

From the very start of instruction, a reading program must be evaluated in respect to all of the aspects of growth desirable for developing a reader who can use reading as a means of mass communication. The unique contribution of reading when compared with other media seems to be that it enables the person to be more critical, to reflect more adequately, to organize more effectively the contributions of many authors, to be more rigorous in thinking with the content of the material, to demand that the authorities consulted be well qualified to express an opinion, and to select authors with whom the reader would like to communicate to fulfill his needs, interests, and desires.

Reading instruction must be broader and more inclusive today than in the past if it is to meet the increasing demands that are being made on the reading abilities of every student. The reading program must do more than develop the basic skills and techniques, although upon these basic skills and techniques the broader goals of the reading program will depend. It must develop more than the ability to group words in language units, even though such grouping enables the reader to become a more fluent and understanding reader than otherwise would be possible. It must develop more than the ability to note details and follow directions, although such comprehension abilities allow the reader to use the printed page in a purposeful manner.

173

The reading program must, in addition, develop broad interest in reading to gain information in many fields, and develop a taste for reading so that the reader can choose material wisely. The program must develop an independent reader, one who can rely upon his own resources, one who will employ self-initiated reading activities, and one who can appraise the reading problems and adjust to the many purposes for reading. It must develop readers who can locate relevant and discard irrelevant material. It must develop readers who are able to see the relationship between things read and the problems they face.

From the start, the program must develop individuals who can rely upon many sources of getting information and who are able to organize their findings from these many sources. It must develop readers who ultimately can distinguish fact and opinion and detect propaganda or prejudice when critical judgments are to be made. Readers must be able to draw conclusions from what has been read. The reading program must develop readers who are able to enjoy reading and who gain from their leisure reading activities a high degree of personal development and satisfaction. It must develop readers who can share interesting materials with others through interpretative oral reading, discussion, and other forms of creative expression.

These, then, are some of the characteristics of a reader who can communicate effectively with authors. The outcomes of the broader reading instruction of today give some guidance in setting up the more specific outcomes of instruction that get their start in the first grades.

Judging Effectiveness

In evaluating a reading program at any level, estimates must be made as to how well the child is growing toward each of the major outcomes of reading instruction, how well the curriculum is organized to achieve these outcomes, and how effective are the methods and materials of instruction in developing the characteristics of independent readers who can communicate with a wide variety of authors for many different purposes. The following questions will help us judge the effectiveness of a reading program:

1. To what extent are the children gaining independence in word recognition? Are the pupils increasing their effectiveness, balance, flexibility, and skill in the following techniques?
   (a) Analyzing words when, and only when, needed.

(b) Developing an adequate sight vocabulary.

(c) Progressing systematically and in an orderly manner from left to right.

(d) Using meaning aids as expectancy clues and checks on accuracy.

(e) Establishing flexibility in visually analyzing words into usable parts.

(f) Increasing knowledge of visual word forms and structural aids.

(g) Gaining in the use of auditory and phonic clues.

(h) Increasing ability to blend words auditorilly and visually.

2. How adequately are the children developing the basic comprehension abilities? Consider how well each child is growing in:

(a) Understanding of word meaning including descriptive words, figures of speech, symbolic expression, and semantic variations.

(b) Techniques of expanding meaning vocabulary, such as: using the author's definition, structural aids to meaning, context clues to meaning, and dictionary definitions.

(c) Understanding sentence organization including thought units, phrasing, sentence sense, and other syntactical aspects of language.

(d) Paragraph meaning and organization including interrelationships among sentences, inductive and deductive order, and the use of topic sentences.

(e) Understanding the relationships among paragraphs.

3. Are the students achieving a well-balanced and adequate growth in various specific comprehension abilities? Consider how well the child is growing in the ability to:

(a) Read for facts which includes the ability to locate and retain specific information and fundamental concepts.

(b) Read to organize which includes the ability to classify and sense relationships between the factual information given within a selection or among selections, to sense a sequence of events, and to follow a series of directions.

(c) Read to evaluate, including such abilities as: judging the reasonableness and relevancy of ideas, sensing implied meanings, and detecting propaganda and bias.

(d) Read to reflect, which includes such abilities as: understanding the general import, drawing an inference or conclusion, predicting outcomes, and forming opinions, or making judgments.

(e) Read to appreciate including the ability to interpret the humor, plot, and action, form sensory impressions, sense the feeling tone, and understand characters.

4. How well are the students able to effectively utilize the basic study skills? To what extent are the following skills being developed at all grade levels?
   (a) Locating information.
   (b) Using general references, such as: picture dictionary, and encyclopedia.
   (c) Interpreting visual materials, such as: charts, maps, graphs, and diagrams.
   (d) Organizing materials, such as: sensing main and subordinate ideas, grouping, and categorizing.
   (e) At the first grade level, instruction in basic study skills is designed to develop readiness for more systematic instruction at more advanced levels.

5. To what extent are the students achieving good oral reading skills? How well is each pupil prepared in the following attributes of oral reading?
   (a) Selecting material that is of interest to the listeners and making the audience feel he wants to share the ideas of the selection.
   (b) Reading as though he were talking, but loud enough for all to hear.
   (c) Reading at a pleasant rate and expressing meaning well.
   (d) Reading in a relaxed, confident manner free from tension.
   (e) Advancing toward the ability to read material with a minimum of preparation.

6. How extensively is the child able to adjust to the demands of the various content fields? Consider the following capabilities in making the evaluation.
   (a) Increasing ability to build the specific background and vocabulary necessary to interpret content material at his level of reading development.
   (b) Developing ability in formulating purposes and adjusting comprehension abilities to meet those purposes suitable to each of the content fields.
   (c) Adjusting rate of comprehension to meet demands of specific content areas.
   (d) Modifying reading to differences in organization found in the materials of the various content fields.

7. To what degree are the children developing desirable habits and attitudes toward reading? How well are all children developing the following important habits and attitudes?

   (a) Understanding that reading is part of written communication and

   (b) Increasing confidence and security in reading situations.

   (c) Appreciating reading as an aid to learning and desiring to satisfy intellectual curiosity by reading.

   (d) Sensing the responsibility of contributing to group enterprises by reading.

   (e) Establishing the habit of reading as a source of enjoyment and demanding an understanding of what is read.

   (f) Seeking self-initiated reading experiences and energetically reading with the intent to learn.

8. How well are the students expanding interests and maturing in taste? How adequately are the following interests and tastes being developed for each pupil?

   (a) Increasing variety of topics about which the child desires to read.

   (b) Increasing the scope of materials of different types, such as: experience charts, stories he knows, and factual and narrative types of material for discovering new ideas.

   (c) Selecting reading for recreational and leisure-time pursuits.

9. How much does the reading program reinforce and extend other phases of the language arts? The following related areas should be considered in making an evaluation of a first grade reading program:

   (a) The quality of independent writing being done by the children.

   (b) The creativity shown in written expression.

   (c) The desire to express oneself in written communication.

   (d) The quality and effectiveness of spoken language.

   (e) The extension of meaning vocabularies in listening, writing, and speaking.

10. To what extent is the child becoming an enthusiastic reader, one who loves books and delights in the wonders unfolded in the whole realm of children's literature? Observations should be made of such characteristics as the following:

    (a) The child's indications of joy in the author's ways of expressing himself.

    (b) The desire to share pleasurable reading experiences with others.

(c) Indications of cherishing certain books as private possessions.

(d) The chuckling over the humor in a book.

(e) The creative interpretation of an imaginative story.

(f) Other evidences of fondness for reading.

Judging Efficiency of Program

In evaluating approaches to first grade reading, we not only need to estimate whether or not they are broad enough to develop all the many capabilities as outlined above but also must consider some other characteristics of the approaches. We should evaluate a reading program from the standpoint of its efficiency in maintaining a balance between and utilizing the opportunities afforded in each of the major types of reading experiences needed to make for maximum growth. We should consider program effectiveness in using the following characteristics of the reading experiences provided throughout the reading curriculum.

1. How well is basic instruction organized so that the skills, abilities and habits are developed in an orderly sequence? In judging consider the following points:
    (a) The program organized so that omissions or overemphases of any skills or abilities are avoided.
    (b) The skills and abilities developed in orderly sequences so that each new learning is introduced only when the prerequisite ones are firmly established.
    (c) The introduction of skills, abilities, and sight vocabularies is well spaced so the load does not become unreasonable.
    (d) Ample repetition of all the learnings given so they may become a permanent part of the readers' equipment.
    (e) Provisions made for differential rates of growth toward the outcomes of reading instruction.

2. In what ways does the curriculum provide for the practice in and the application of the maturing reading skills, abilities and habits? Consideration should be given to the following opportunities:
    (a) Units to extend topics introduced in the reading program which are employed generously.
    (b) Enrichment by extensive reading of topics dealt with in content areas frequently used.
    (c) Provisions made for reading instruction which refine and extend the specific skills and abilities related to each content field.

(d) Independent reading of recreational and personal development materials encouraged and school time allotted for such reading.

3. How well does the curriculum provide for those children encountering reading difficulties? Such provisions as the following should be judged:
   (a) The activities of the reading curriculum are organized so that the teacher can work with small groups with specific reading needs while the rest of the class is working independently.
   (b) The reading curriculum is suitable and encouraging to children of varied reading capacities.
   (c) The curriculum provides opportunities for all the children, irrespective of reading capabilities, to contribute to the various class enterprises.
   (d) The curriculum provides for means of studying instructional needs of the children in reading difficulties.
   (e) The curriculum utilizes materials and methods suited to correcting reading defects.

In addition to the total curriculum considerations, we should evaluate the approaches to reading in regard to certain questions we should raise about the flexibility in methods and use of materials. Such questions as the following should be given careful consideration:

1. How effectively are all available sources of information used by teachers in assessing the reading attainments' of the pupils? Consider the following:
   (a) Adequate cumulative records which are kept and used.
   (b) Systematic testing programs which include at least appraisals of various reading skills, mental ability, vision and hearing screening tests.
   (c) Diagnostic testing programs which are utilized in the classroom as well as in remedial centers.
   (d) Teacher appraisals which are used to supplement other evaluations.
   (e) All appraisals interrelated to understand the pupils' instructional needs.

2. How adequately do the instructional procedures provide for individual differences? The following should be appraised:
   (a) Current plans of providing for individual differences have been

studied and evaluated in terms of the school's organization, facilities, and the educational merit of the plans.

(b) Grouping procedures are used which are flexible, practical, and based upon the personal needs of the child.

(c) Instruction based upon reading levels of the child.

(d) Instruction adapted to reading needs as revealed by continuous classroom diagnostic procedures.

3. To what extent is proper use made of instructional aids? Consider the following points:

   (a) Teachers manuals studied and the suggested procedures intelligently adapted to the children's needs.

   (b) Workbooks and other seat work which aids in the teaching and diagnosis of reading skills.

   (c) Teacher's procedures that encourage wide use of supplementary materials.

   (d) Teacher constructs material to meet specific reading needs.

   (e) Teacher makes frequent and effective use of visual aids in the reading program.

4. To what extent are these fundamental instructional procedures applied in the reading program and the content fields? To what degree are these procedures followed?

   (a) Teacher makes classroom environment conducive to reading growth.

   (b) Teacher carefully prepares for each lesson and unit of reading instruction.

   (c) Teacher adequately develops interest, background, and vocabulary for every reading situation.

   (d) Reading purposes are set before reading.

   (e) Teacher gives systematic instruction in how selection should be read.

   (f) Re-reading to develop specific skills and abilities is done as needed.

   (g) Drills on skills and abilities are utilized as needed.

   (h) Creative activities are an integral part of the reading program.

   (i) Evaluation is constantly employed by teacher and the pupils.

5. How adequately are the teachers incorporating diversified methods into the instructional program? Such types of instruction as the following should be apparent and appropriately used:

   (a) Experience charts which introduce reading in a meaningful setting.

(b) Oral study methods which, when used sparingly, give the child help in word recognition and give the teacher diagnostic opportunities.

(c) Silent reading methods which encourage a wide range of comprehension abilities.

(d) Word recognition methods, including visual, structural, and contextual aids, and sight word methods.

(e) Problem solving and purposeful reading methods centered about units through which a variety of comprehension and basic study skills are developed.

6. How carefully are teachers avoiding methods which are detrimental to present growth or limit future development in reading? Practices such as the following should be avoided:

(a) Round-the-room oral reading of texts at any level of instruction.

(b) Letter-by-letter spelling or letter-by-letter sounding methods of word recognition.

(c) Complete dependence upon any one instructional approach.

(d) Dependence upon interest alone or "lush environment" methods to develop balanced reading skills and abilities.

7. How well supplied are the classrooms with materials essential for an effective reading program? Are the following types of materials made abundantly available and suited to the range of reading abilities in the classroom?

(a) At all grade levels, textbooks for basic instruction in reading, including teachers manuals and skill development books.

(b) Textbooks for systematic presentation in the various content fields.

(c) Supplementary books for expansion of units in both the basic reading program and the content fields.

(d) Recreational and personal development reading including selections from the finest children's literature.

(e) Reference books related to all aspects of the reading curriculum.

(f) Other library books and materials in a well supplied central library.

(g) Audio-visual aid materials of all types suitably used to extend and enrich the entire reading program.

(h) Materials developed by teachers to meet specific instructional needs.

(i) Materials essential for thorough appraisal of the reading needs and achievements of the pupils.

Conference Evaluation

Making an evaluation of the conference we have just completed is indeed a difficult task. It is obvious that we have listened to and discussed a wide variety of the most outstanding papers it has been anyone's privilege to hear in the field of reading. We have heard about a group of approaches to reading supported by conscientious and able scholars in areas in which they are well informed and in which they have done considerable thinking. We can, therefore, do nothing but evaluate the overall excellency of this conference in glowing terms.

We must, however, make certain observations in respect to the various approaches to first grade reading that have been discussed. Among the most important of these is that although there is much that is different in the approaches to reading, there is also much that is similar. Often the differences are in the nature of emphasis rather than in uniqueness.

The approaches have many rudimentary characteristics in common. All the approaches, for example, have indicated concern about instructional procedures that make possible adjustments to individual rates of learning, individual interests, and instructional needs of children. There were apparent, however, varying amounts of concern about these problems and different suggested techniques for implementing such adjustments. We have discussed these adjustments as suggested by individualized programs, language experience approaches and basal reader programs. From a consideration of the over all problem, including adjustment not only to interest and levels of attainment but also to instructional needs, it is difficult to evaluate the comparative effectiveness of the techniques suggested in any of the approaches. In this, as in many other respects, the greatest weakness in our discussion was in the area of experimental evidence brought to bear upon the problem not because the discussants did not give the evidence available but because such experimental evidence is sparse. This is partly true because the teaching techniques discussed have been clearly defined only recently and, therefore, have not been subjected to as thorough research as we would like.

Another observation that can be made about the approaches to reading presented is that all focused upon important outcomes of reading instruction but with varying emphasis and with differing concerns about the necessary balance among the outcomes. For example, certain phonic approaches discussed seemed to show little concern for developing rapid word recognition techniques and building a vocabulary of rapid recognition words. Many of the meaning aids to word recognition seem to be neglected and the importance of basic comprehension abilities appear to be relegated to a secondary place of emphasis. Of course it should be pointed out that many phonic approaches are not usually thought of as being self sufficient but as a corollary to a broader, more diversified reading program. Dr. Heilman emphasized in his paper that most programs have strong phonic components and that most phonics programs are designed to supplement other approaches to reading. It is only when a phonics program attempts to become an end in itself that difficulties in overall reading growth may be expected to ensue.

The proper balance among the various outcomes of reading instruction is one that needs careful investigation. It would appear, for example, that individualized programs do not afford sufficient structure to maintain a skills program nor to develop basic comprehension abilities. They appear to focus upon personal reading and development of reading interest and to somewhat neglect the development of skills and abilities. The linguistic approaches described seem to focus on word forms and language patterns so intently that interest in personal reading and the need for preparing children to read in the rest of the curriculum appear to be neglected. Careful, well-controlled research investigating which instructional outcomes are achieved and which are neglected will be needed before an accurate evaluation of these approaches can be made.

Another observation that can be made is that an approach that looks similar to another approach at a casual glance proves to be so different in fundamental points that it is, in reality, closer to still a third approach. For example, the language experience approach described by Russell Stauffer would appear to be closely related to the individualized reading approach suggested by Patrick Groff. Indeed it is in some respects but in others and maybe in the more fundamental respects, it is closer to the basal reader approach described by William Sheldon. It is true that Dr. Stauffer used dictated stories, creative writing, and individual reading experience approaches in many of his introductory reading lessons, but he also accompanied these experiences with a well-structured skill development program for a half-hour a day. As the children developed in reading, they read in primer materials independently and later they were given group instruction using basal first grade readers. Dr. Sheldon, in describing the basal reader approach, used experience charts as a means of transition from prereading language experience to basal materials. Then as the children received instruction in basal readers, he reinforced the programs with many language experiences including creative writing and self-selective reading opportunities. Again, there is evidence that we need research to tell us for what kind of children and for which outcomes each of the approaches is best suited.

We need to know the emphasis that will make for maximum growth by children differing in perceptual characteristics, in linguistic capabilities, in culturally differing environments, and in learning capacities. It is on a basis of such knowledge that differential instruction can be given. We also need to know when a child is growing in reading capability in an unfortunate pattern so that diagnostic teaching using the appropriate emphasis to overcome his problem can be undertaken.

This year the conference on perspectives has presented a variety of reading approaches, all of which warrant careful scientific investigation. Such investigation is now underway in the First Grade Reading Studies being sponsored by the Cooperative Research Division of the United States Office of Education. These studies are, in fact, twenty-seven independent studies so well coordinated in research design, instruments of measurement, information gathered, and comparability of data collected that comparisons among the studies will be possible in ways that have not previously existed. The most unique characteristic of the First Grade Reading Project is that it can also be considered one large study since all of the data obtained in the twenty-seven individual studies will be fed into a Coordinating Center for combined analysis, enabling the testing of many hypotheses that are not within the scope of any one of the independent studies nor in any comparison of the independent findings between the studies.

We hope to get answers to many of the questions raised in the conference on perspectives since all of the approaches to reading that have been presented to this conference are included in the First Grade Reading Studies as experimental variables. We, for the first time, have the opportunity of studying the efficiency of these approaches in a variety of school populations and under instructional conditions all so well controlled that each aspect can be studied in detail. This project involves nearly 30,000 children and 1,000 teachers in a variety of communities. The following list of experimental variables being studied indicates the scope of the enterprise and the number of individual projects in which each variable is included as one of the several approaches to reading:

Basal Reader 24
Language Experience 12
Phonic Emphasis 6
Linguistic Emphasis 6
New Alphabet 5
Early Letter Approach 4
Individualized Reading 4
Reading Readiness 4
Audio-Visual 4
Teacher Supervisor 4
Approaches for Culturally Different 5
Other Approaches 7

The data from the combined studies will be analyzed, wherever possible, with special attention to locating the pupil characteristics associated with success in each of the many approaches to teaching reading represented in the independent studies. Specifically, such analyses will study the effectiveness of the various approaches to teaching reading for children with high, average, or low intelligence, readiness, auditory perception, visual perception, etc., and any interaction that may take place between the methods represented in the individual studies and such pupil characteristics. Studies of this type never have been possible previously in such scope. The various methods of first grade reading represented in the individual projects will be compared to find out the comparative effectiveness of each in producing each type of reading growth represented in the common dependent variables. This phase of the study will have importance in assessing the contribution the various individual approaches might have in a combination approach to reading instruction.

In order to improve reading instruction, it also will be necessary for reading research workers to enlist the aid of other experts in areas related to the teaching of reading. We should work closely with the perceptual and experimental psychologists, with linguists, sociologists, clinical and learning psychologists, neurologists, and sensory specialists to name a few. Such cooperative endeavors are now capable of accomplishing understanding heretofore impossible. Modern research techniques and equipment allow for tremendous advances in the study of such complex problems as are involved in the field of reading in all of its aspects.